Art Center College Library
1700 Lida Street
Pasadena, CA 91103

ART CENTER COLLEGE OF DESIGN

3 3220 00282 8312

659.2850945
S559
2008
c.2

Art Center College Library
1700 Lida Street
Pasadena, CA 91103

Short'N'Strong

PROJECT CONCEPT CREATED BY
Kalimera

×××××××××××××××××××××××××××××

COLLECTED AND SELECTED BY
Red Publishing

×××××××××××××××××××××××××××××

DESIGNED AND EDITED BY
Kalimera

×××××××××××××××××××××××××××××

ENGLISH TRANSLATION BY
Antonietta Di Sciuva

×××××××××××××××××××××××××××××

PRINTED BY
Grafiche Siz
Verona, Italy

×××××××××××××××××××××××××××××

RED PUBLISHING. 2008
ISBN 978-88-88492-10-0

×××××××××××××××××××××××××××××

© RED PUBLISHING.
Modena, Italy.
All rights reserved.
No part of this publication
may be reproduced or transmitted
in any form or by any means,
electronic or mechanical,
including photocopy or any storage
and retrieval system,
without permission in writing
from the publisher.

Red Publishing
Viale Prampolini, 110
41100 Modena Italy
phone + 39.059.212792
fax +39.059.4392133
www.redonline.it
info@redonline.it

From graphic design to identity design

After the experimentations of the 90s, world design for visual communication has come to a great cultural maturity, going beyond its mere aesthetic role. The same has happened to Italian graphic design: based on a long artistic tradition, it has been deeply influenced by this global evolution.

And yet worldwide, in the collective imagination the Italian design is still mainly associated to industry and fashion, whereas Italian creativity goes far beyond. Actually, as this book shows, the design of our "bel Paese" has gained a considerable importance at international level, without giving up its unique style, which is recognizable in the formal essentiality, in the elegant chromatic associations, in the masterly usage of typeface.

This goal has been reached also thanks to Italian companies, who have become increasingly aware of the importance of visual identity, of corporate culture and of the value a brand has in today's highly competitive market.

Compared to times past, graphic design has recently gained a strategic importance in the making of corporate identity, to an extent that it is more and more frequent to find a new professional with specific skills: the identity designer.

This new professional plays a key role in the consolidation of a brand and of its message, as opposed to its competitors. The role of identity is to make the brand stand out in the visual noise of contemporary world and to identify a company or service in a clear, straightforward, memorable way.

And then there is the emotional component of identity. The bigger the emotional factor of a brand, the bigger its appeal to the consumers.

When creating a new visual identity, it is basic to give iconography its proper tactical value. The quantity of information a logo can convey and the probability of being memorized depend largely on its technical and visual structure. Creativity alone is not enough, it is necessary to add a careful analysis of forms, based on a scrupulous study on how our brain receives and elaborates information. This is the only way, for example, to create an "iconbrand" – as I call it - that is, a symbol which, thanks to its remarkable personality, can lead a brand to success.

An "iconbrand" is original, peculiar, not abstract – think to the Apple logo – it is immediately recognizable, both in its language and in its form. The human intellect tends to break down complex items into sums of simple items, and this must be the starting point for studying a new identity: the fewer associative steps are necessary to break down the compositions into familiar forms, the easier for the brand to stick in the consumer's mind.

The emotional component is therefore one of the main fun-ctions of a logo, not only with regards to the conceptual coherence with the relevant brand, but basically and simply for highlighting its own distinctiveness. When a graphic symbol can engender a comparison with something already existing in the consumer's mind, then that symbol can be classified and recorded by the unconscious.

When coming to identity, it goes without saying that visual message should not be just "beautiful", but perfectly functional, so to turn a logo into a brand.

Gaetano Grizzanti
Brand Identity Designer.
Professor of Aesthetics
of the Brand at the Brescia Academy of Fine Arts.

Short'N'Strong

TASTE THE REAL ITALIAN
CORPORATE IDENTITY!

xxxxxxxxxxxxxxxxxxxxxxxxxxxxxxxx

❯008❮

×××

agency/design studio	client	art director
Zetalab	Esterni	Lucio LuZo Lazzara

designer	year
Walter Molteni	2007

> 010 <

×××

agency/design studio	client	art director
2mlab	Bibò	Mirko Magnani

designer	year
Mirko Magnani	2005

agency/design studio	client	art director
2mlab	Meanwhile	Mirko Magnani

designer	year	
Mirko Magnani	2006	

>012<

xxxxxxxxxxxxxxxxxxxxxxxxxxxxxxxxxxxxxxxxxxxxxxxxxxxxxxxxxxxxxxxxxxxxxxxxxxxxxxxxxxx

agency/design studio	client	art director
Happycentro	**Nike**	**Giuliano Garonzi**

× × × × × ×

× × × × × ×

designer	year
Giuliano Garonzi	**2007**

× × × × × ×

× × × × × ×

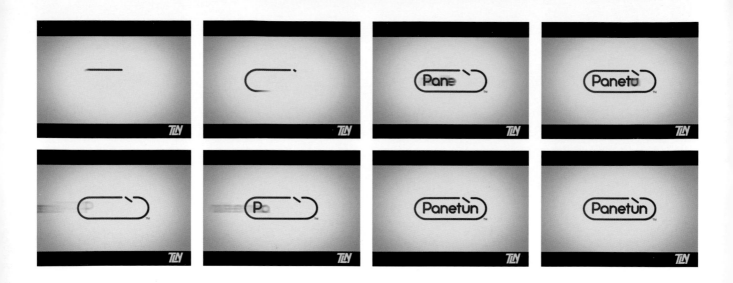

CAMPIÓN DEL MÓND, CAMPIÓN DE L'EUROPA, CAMPIÓN DE L'ITALIA.

MADUNINA UNITED
LA PUSSÉE FORTA CHE GH'È

>015<

agency/design studio	client	art director
Happycentro	Nike	Giuliano Garonzi

designers	year
Giuliano Garonzi; Massimo Soprano	2007

> **016** ◄

×××

agency/design studio		client		art director	
Happycentro		Nike		Giuliano Garonzi	
×	×	×	×	×	×
×	×	×	×	×	×
designer		year			
Giuliano Garonzi		2007			
				×	×
×	×	×	×	×	×
×	×	×	×	×	×

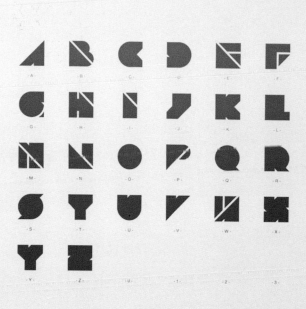

- JUVENTUS ALPHABET -

SWITCH™
HIGH PERFORMANCE BIKES

>018<

×××

agency/design studio	client	art director
2mlab	Switch	Mirko Magnani

designer	year
Mirko Magnani	2006

>020◀

×××

agency/design studio		client		art director	
Basaglia.com		Astra Casinò		Fausto Basaglia	
×	×	×		×	×	×
×	×	×		×		×
designer		year			
Fausto Basaglia		2002/2004		×		×
×	×	×		×		×
×	×	×		×		×

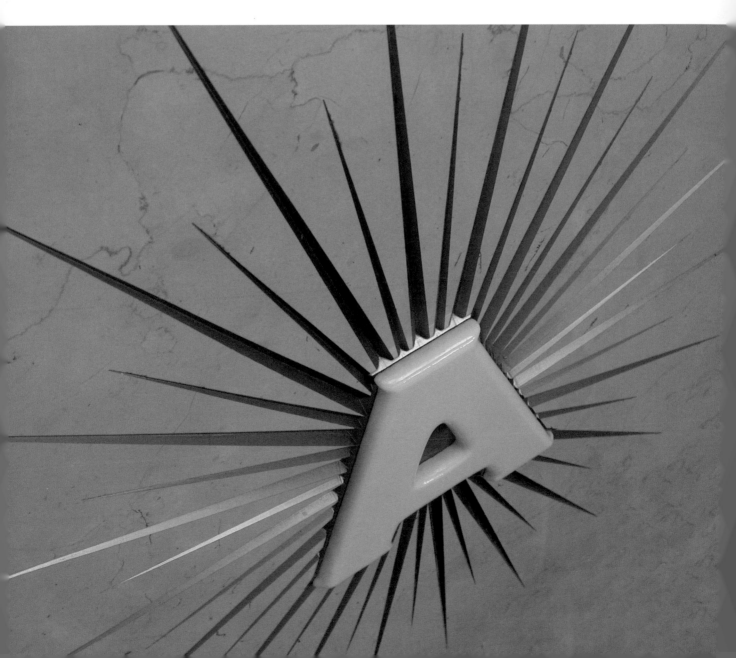

×××

agency/design studio	client	art director
Stockbridge	**Casino Royale**	**Stockbridge**
designer	year	
Stockbridge	**2006**	

Brian Had
A Little Plate

EL GALLO ROJO
R E C O R D S

>024<

agency/design studio	client	art directors
Massimiliano Sorrentini	El Gallo Rojo	Massimiliano Sorrentini Sara Meneghini

designer	year	
Massimiliano Sorrentini	2006/2007	

xxxxxxxxxxxxxxxxxxxxxxxxxxxxxxxxxxxxxxxxxxxxxxxxxxxxxxxxxxxxxxxxxxxxxxxxx

agency/design studio		client		art director	
Kalimera		Vodafone		1861 United	
×	×	×	×	×	×
×	×	×	×	×	×
designer		year			
Kalimera		2007/2008		×	
×	×	×	×	×	×
×	×	×	×	×	×

agency/design studio	client	art director
Longe Design	Fornari Spa (Combo/ComboBELLA)	Heric Longe Abramo
designer	year	
Heric Longe Abramo	2005	

xx

agency/design studio	client	art director	
Longe Design	**Fornari Spa (Combo/ComboBELLA)**	**Heric Longe Abramo**	
x	x	x	x
x	x	x	x
designer	year	x	x
Heric Longe Abramo	**2005**		
x	x	x	x
x	x	x	x

Combo Graphic Series
a collaboration between Combo
and the best graphic designers
celebrating the world of graphics.

Combo Graphic Series:
una collaborazione tra Combo
ed i migliori graphic designer per
celebrare il mondo della grafica.

Combo Italian Street Style since 1995.

www.comboit

COMBO
graphic series?
23
MEDIUM
Made in Italy

COMBO

COMBO
graphic series?
23
MEDIUM
Made in Italy

COMBO
graphic series?
23
MEDIUM
Made in

xxx

agency/design studio	client	art director
Copiaincolla	Copiaincolla	Cesare Tonolli

designer	year
Cesare Tonolli	2007

Art Center College Library
1700 Lida Street
Pasadena, CA 91103

>036<

×××

agency/design studio	client	art director
Startmedia	IISE	Anna Mercurio
	Istituto Italiano per gli Studi Europei	

designer	year
Anna Mercurio	2006/2007

*i*se
istituto italiano
per gli studi europei

❯038❮

×××

agency/design studio		client		art director	
Studio Sancisi		**1000 Piedi Polisportivattiva**		**Nicola Sancisi**	
×	×	×	×	×	×
×	×	×	×	×	×
designer		year			
Laura Testasecca		**2007**		×	×
×	×	×	×	×	×
×	×	×	×	×	×

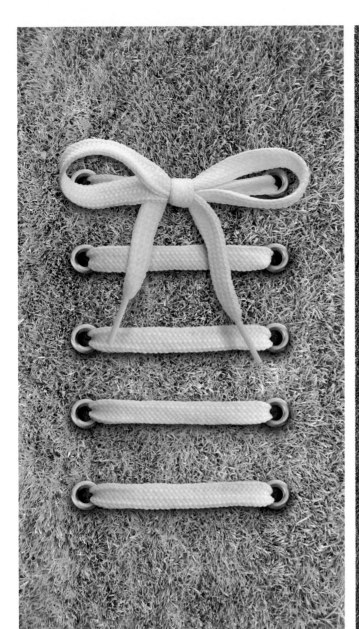

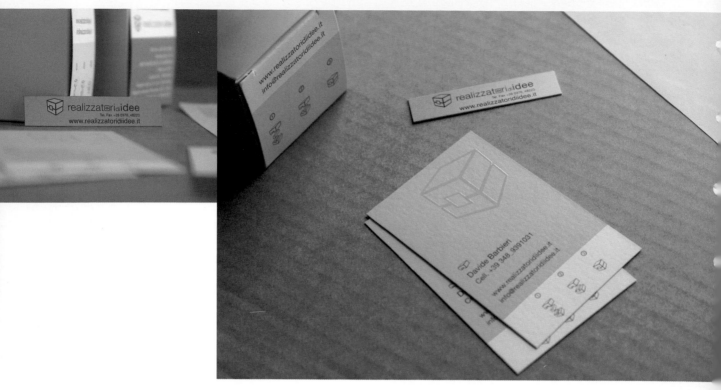

realizzat◻ri di idee

×××

agency/design studio	client	art director
Copiaincolla	Realizzatori di idee	Cesare Tonolli

designer	year
Elena Cottignoli	2005

> 042 <
xxxxxxxxxxxxxxxxxxxxxxxxxxxxxxxxxxxxxxxxxxxxxxxxxxxxxxxxxxxxxxxxxxxxxxxxxxxxxxxxxxxx

agency/design studio		client		art directors	
R&MAG		Liu-Jo luxury		Raffaele Fontanella	
				Maurizio Di Somma	
×	×	×	×	Marcello Cesar	
×	×	×	×	×	×
designers		year			
Raffaele Fontanella		2006		×	×
Maurizio Di Somma					
Marcello Cesar		×	×	×	×
×	×	×	×	×	×

>043<
xxxxxxxxxxxxxxxxxxxxxxxxxxxxxxxxxxxxxxxxxxxxxxxxxxxxxxxxxxxxxxxxxxxxxxxxxxxxxxxxxxxx

agency/design studio	client	art director
Creativamente	**Creativamente**	**Giovanni Amato**
×	×	×
×	×	×
designer	year	
Giovanni Amato	**2006**	
×	×	×
×	×	×

>044◀

agency/design studio	client	art director		
Up!	Be-atitud	Up!		
×	× ×	× ×	×
×	× ×	× ×	×
designer	year	×	×
Up!	2006	×	×
×	× ×	× ×	×
×	× ×	× ×	×

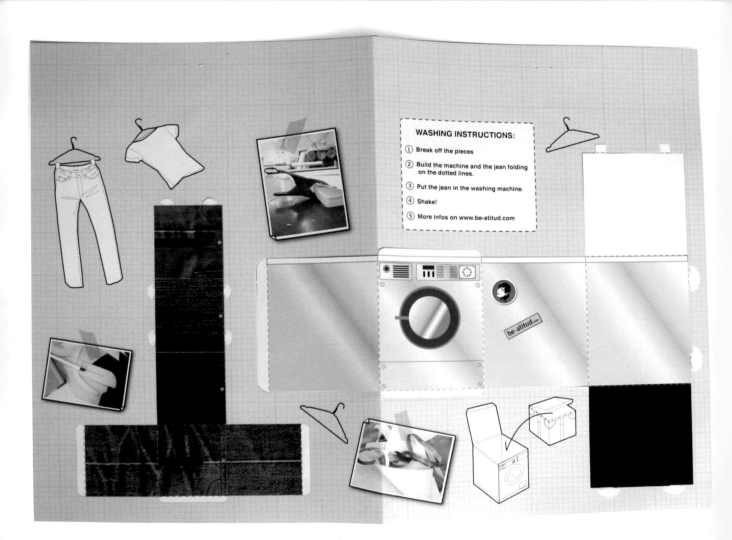

WASHING INSTRUCTIONS:

① Break off the pieces

② Build the machine and the jean folding on the dotted lines.

③ Put the jean in the washing machine.

④ Shake!

⑤ More infos on www.be-atitud.com

xx

agency/design studio		client		art director		
Up!		400gr		Up!		
×	×	×		×	×	×
×	×	×		×	×	×
designer		year			×	×
Up!		2006				
×	×	×		×	×	×
×	×	×		×	×	×

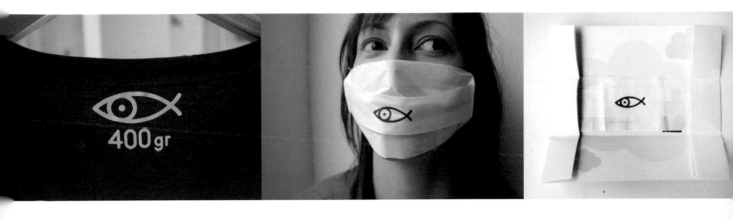

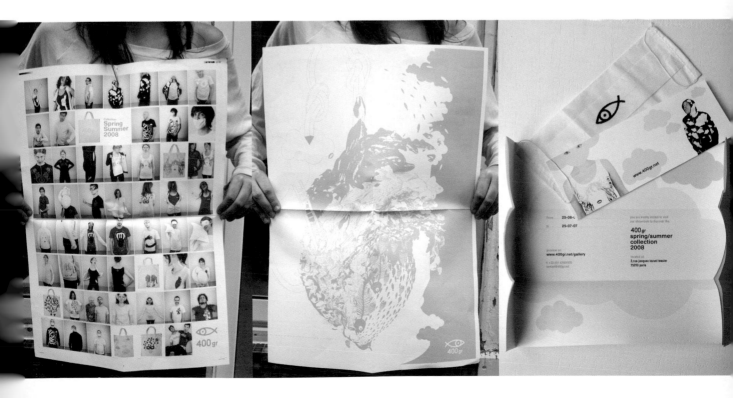

xxx

agency/design studio		client		art director	
Fabbricando		CMC Ravenna		Claudia Fabbri	
×	×	×	×	×	×
×	×	×	×	×	×
designer		year			
Claudia Fabbri		2005		×	×
×	×	×	×	×	×
×	×	×	×	×	×

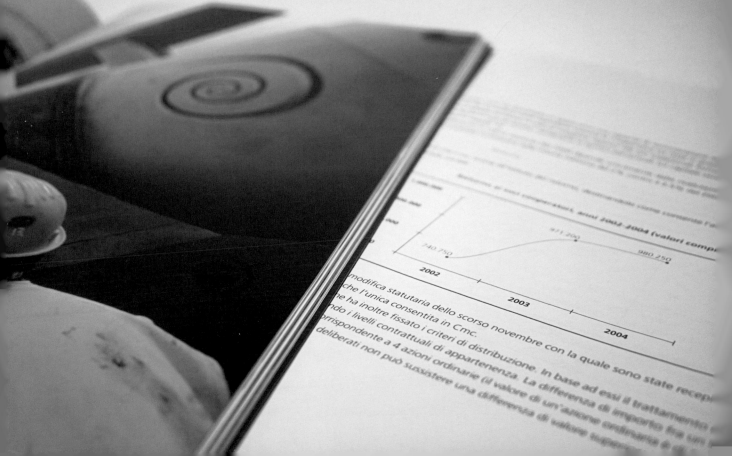

❯047❮

×××

agency/design studio		client		art director	
Fabbricando		**CMC Ravenna**		**Claudia Fabbri**	
×	×	×	×	×	×
×	×	×	×	×	×
designer		year			
Claudia Fabbri		**2005**			
				×	×
×	×	×	×	×	×
×	×	×	×	×	×

talia
phone

servizi per telefonia mobile

❯049❮

×××

agency/design studio	client	art director
Fabbricando	**Talia srl**	**Claudia Fabbri**

×   × ×   × ×   ×

×   × ×   × ×   ×

designers	year	
Claudia Fabbri	**2006**	×
Jonas Severi		

×   × ×   × ×   ×

×   × ×   × ×   ×

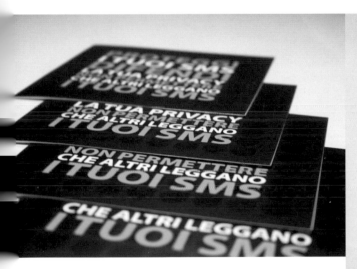

tesei legno

❯050❮

×××

agency/design studio	client	art director
Fabbricando	**Tesei legno**	**Claudia Fabbri**

× × × × ×

× × × × ×

designer	year
Claudia Fabbri	**2006**	× ×

× × × × ×

× × × × ×

tesei jader via mariana 530
47023 martorano cesena fc

mobile +39 348 9587087
partita iva 03491320408

tesei legno

posatore strutture in legno
e arredamento per esterno

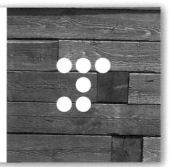

tesei jader via mariana 530
47023 martorano cesena fc

mobile +39 348 9587087
partita iva 03491320408

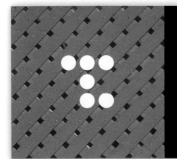

tesei legno

posatore strutture in legno
e arredamento per esterno

tesei jader via mariana 530
47023 martorano cesena fc

mobile +39 348 9587087
partita iva 03491320408

××

agency/design studio	client	art director
Copiaincolla	**Quality consulting**	**Cesare Tonolli**

× × × × × ×

× × × × × ×

designer	year
Cesare Tonolli	**2005**

× × ×

× × × × × ×

× × × × × ×

STUDIO · MAGISTRELLI · SAVOIA

QUALITY CONSULTING

Q

QUALITY CONSULTING

Consulenza per sistemi di organizzazione aziendale **Quality Consulting** di Magistrelli V. e Savoia C. s.n.c.
Via SS Martiri 2/B · 46100 Mantova · tel. e fax 0376/328753 · info@studiomagistrellisavoia.it · www.studiomagistrellisavoia.it · P. IVA 02100490206

Chiara Savoia
chiara@studiomagistrellisavoia.it
tel. e fax 0376/328753
info@studiomagistrellisavoia.it
www.studiomagistrellisavoia.it
P. IVA 02100490206

STUDIO · MAGISTRELLI · SAVOIA
QUALITY CONSULTING
Q

QUALITY CONSULTING
Q

Consulenza per sistemi
di organizzazione aziendale
Quality Consulting
di Magistrelli V. e Savoia C. s.n.c.
Via SS Martiri 2/B · 46100 Mantova

xx

agency/design studio	client	art director
Akuna Matata	Benedini verde	Miriam Eise

designer	year
Giuseppe Lucchetti	2006

××

agency/design studio		client		art director	
Akuna Matata		Casolaro Spa		Giuseppe Lucchetti	
×	×	×	×	×	×
×	×	×	×		×
designer		year		×	×
Giuseppe Lucchetti		2006			
×	×	×	×	×	×
×	×	×	×	×	×

×××

agency/design studio		client	art director	
Oikos Associati sas		Castadiva pictures	Isabella Garlati	
×	×	×	×	×
×	×	×	×	×
designer		year	×	×
Isabella Garlati		2005		
×	×	×	×	×
×	×	×	×	×

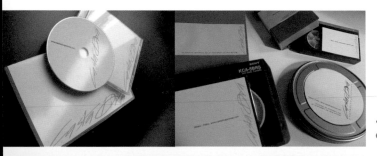

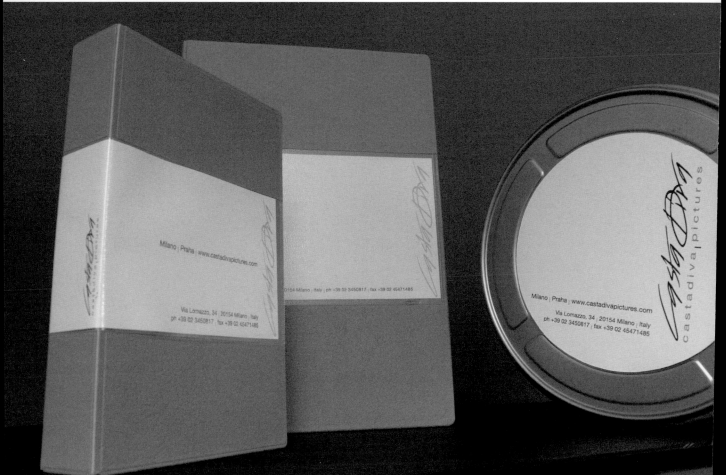

×××

agency/design studio	client	art director	
Andrea Amadio	**GB Group srl**	**Andrea Amadio**	
×	× ×	× ×	×
×	× ×	× ×	×
designer	year		
Andrea Amadio	**2006**	×	×
×	× ×	× ×	×
×	× ×	× ×	×

××

agency/design studio	client	design director
Univisual - Milan	Salmoiraghi e Viganò (optical store chain_ italian leader)	Gaetano Grizzanti
×	× ×	× ×
×	× ×	× ×
designers	year	
Gaetano Grizzanti; Sara Villa; Maurizio Strippoli	2004	× ×
×	× ×	× ×
×	× ×	× ×

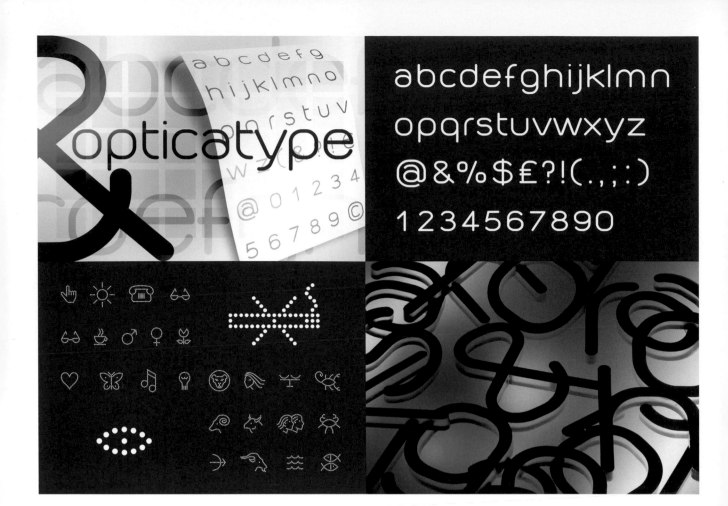

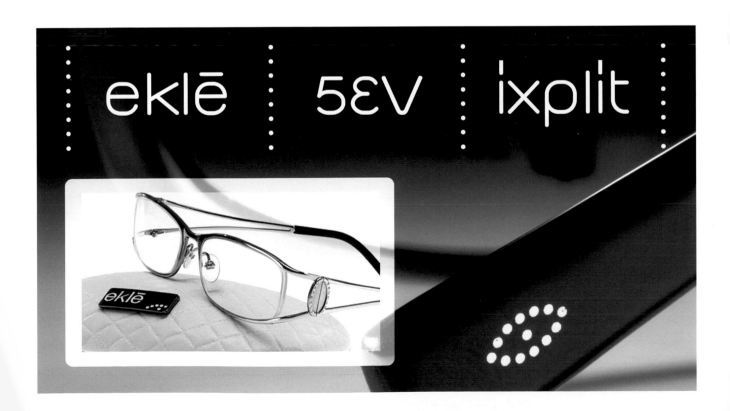

>062<

××

agency/design studio		client		art director		
Zetalab		Esterni		Lucio LuZo Lazzara		
×	×	×		×	×	×
×	×	×		×	×	×
designer		year				
Walter Molteni		2006				
				×		×
×	×	×		×		×
×	×	×		×	×	×

×××

agency/design studio	client	art director
FK Design Srl	Wish	Federico Frasson

×	× ×	× ×	×
×	× ×	× ×	×

designer	year		
Federico Frasson	2005	×	×

×	× ×	× ×	×
×	× ×	× ×	×

×××

agency/design studio	client	art director
FK Design Srl	**Il Gufo Spa**	**Giovanni Frison**

× × × × × ×

× × × × × ×

designer	year	
Giovanni Frison	**2005**	

× × × × ×

× × × × × ×

ABCDEFGHIJI LMNOPQRSTUVWXYZ
1234567890

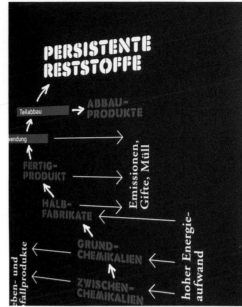

xxxxxxxxxxxxxxxxxxxxxxxxxxxxxxxxxxxxxxxxxxxxxxxxxxxxxxxxxxxxxxxxxxxxxxxxxx

agency/design studio		client		art director	
Alexander Egger		Designforum		Alexander Egger	
x	x	x	x	x	x
x	x	x	x	x	x
designer		year			
Alexander Egger		2007			
				x	x
x	x	x	x	x	x
x	x	x	x	x	x

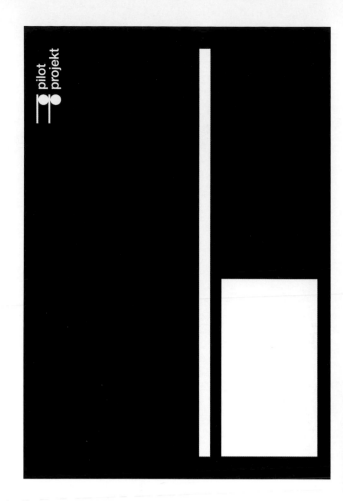

××

agency/design studio	client	art director
Alexander Egger	**Pilotprojekt**	**Alexander Egger**

| × | | × | | × | × | | × |

| × | | × | × | | × | × | | × |

designer	year			
Alexander Egger	**2007**			

× | × | | | × | | × |

| × | | × | × | | × | × | | × |

| × | | × | × | | × | × | | × |

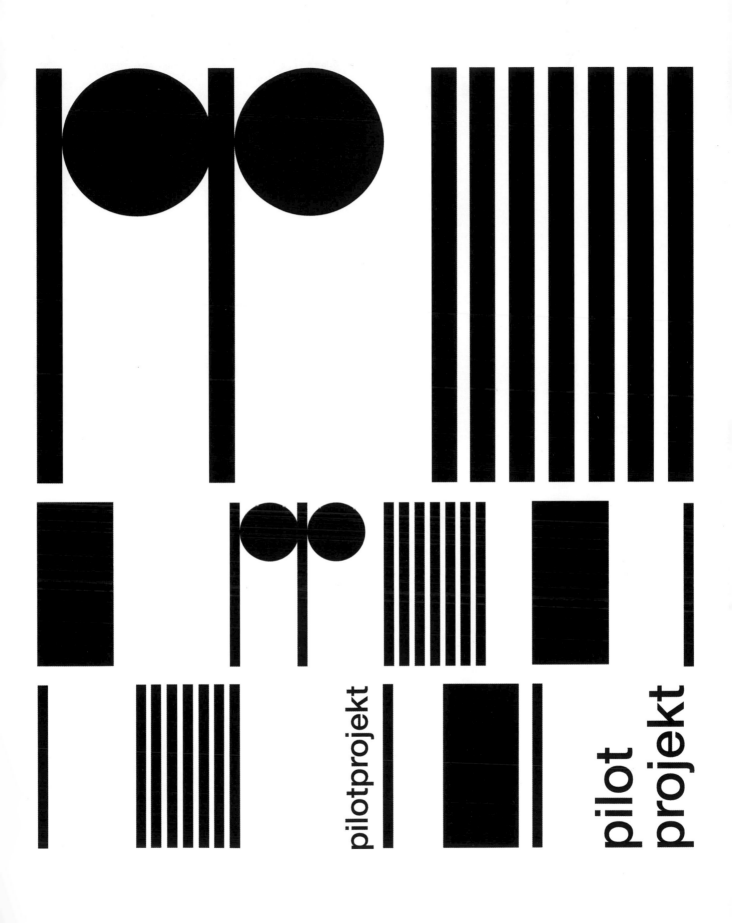

pilotprojekt

pilot
projekt

>070<

agency/design studio		client		art director		
X-ray		Granulati Italia S.p.A.		Paolo Galimberti		
×	×	×		×	×	×
×	×	×		×	×	×
designer		year				
Paolo Galimberti		2005				
				×		×
×	×	×		×	×	×
×	×	×		×	×	×

G-POWER

Il gelato
energizzante

xxxxxxxxxxxxxxxxxxxxxxxxxxxxxxxxxxxxxxxxxxxxxxxxxxxxxxxxxxxxxxxxxxxxxxxxxxxxxxxxxxxxxxxxxxxxxxxxxxxx

agency/design studio	client	art director
FK Design Srl	**Associazione Culturale Veneto Jazz**	**Giovanni Frison**

designer	year
Giovanni Frison	**2006/2007**

EUROMEET
JAZZ FESTIVAL

Magazine

2 LUGLIO < 24 AGOSTO 2003

VENETOJAZZ
15°
1988 2003
ANNIVERSARY

Jazz

Guida al festival

VENETO JAZZ

REGIONE DEL VENETO
giunta regionale

Ministero per i Beni
e le Attività Culturali

×××

agency/design studio	client	art director	
FK Design Srl	Perlanera Srl	Federico Frasson	
×	×	×	×
×	×	×	×
designer	year	×	×
Federico Frasson	2005/2007	×	×
×	×	×	×
×	×	×	×

>078◀

agency/design studio		client		art director	
FK Design Srl		Arte Zurlo Spa		Federico Frasson	
×	×	×	×	×	×
×	×	×	×	×	×
designer		year			×	×
Federico Frasson		2005		×	×
×	×	×	×	×	×
×	×	×	×	×	×

ALMAPLENA

ALMAPLENA
DREAM YOURSELF

Nonostante quel suo sogno
fosse stato popolato da un'infinità
di persone, di luoghi, di colori
e di oggetti così veri da poterne sentire,
attento sfiorandoli, la loro materia,
nonostante ciò sapeva
che il tutto prendeva vigore e vibrava
solo perché lei era viva
che solo ne era testimone.

×××

agency/design studio		client		art director	
Fabbricando		Mingozzi modi d'arredare		Claudia Fabbri	
×	×	×	×	×	×
×	×	×	×	×	×
designer		year			×
Claudia Fabbri		2004		×	
×	×	×	×	×	
×	×	×	×	×	

×××

agency/design studio	client	art director
FK Design Srl	Benipharma World	Giovanni Frison

designer	year
Giovanni Frison	2006

agency/design studio	client	art director
[mu]design	Musei civici di Imola	Mannes Laffi

designers	year	
Vladimiro Bendandi	2006	
Mannes Laffi		

MUSICA

agency/design studio	client	art director	
Studio Priori & C. di Priori Roberto ss	Comune di Palermo	Roberto Priori	
×	× ×	× ×	×
×	× ×	× ×	×
designer	year	×	×
Roberto Priori	2005/2006		
×	× ×	× ×	×
×	× ×	× ×	×

Kals'art musica

"Kals'art Musica" torna alla Kalsa, nei luoghi simbolo del quartiere, per creare un percorso artistico trasversale che, in piena tradizione Kals'art, vede commistioni tra generi molto diversi tra loro, dal folk al jazz, dall'elettronica al rock.
La manifestazione, come sempre, è l'occasione per scoprire artisti che, in vario modo, si sono fatti notare nel panorama musicale: un'occasione per frequentare spettacoli ed attività artistiche diffuse nel resto d'Italia e d'Europa, ma anche un palcoscenico per alcuni tra i più qualificati musicisti della città.
Cuore dell'edizione 2006 è il progetto Alavò, un concerto dedicato alle ninna nanne della tradizione siciliana, che vede coinvolte alcune tra le più belle voci dialettali dell'isola in un percorso che unisce artiste ormai consolidate e nuove pro-

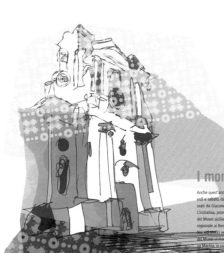

I monumenti della Kalsa

Anche quest'anno, da venerdì 21 luglio a venerdì 15 settembre, ogni giovedì, venerdì e sabato, dalle 21 alle 24, sarà possibile visitare musei, chiese e oratori decorati da Giacomo Serpotta che si trovano all'interno del perimetro della Kalsa. L'iniziativa, promossa dal Comune, è in collaborazione con l'associazione Amici dei Musei siciliani, l'Università degli Studi, l'Arcidiocesi di Palermo, l'assessorato regionale ai Beni culturali e la Soprintendenza dei Beni Culturali.
Nei vari luoghi verranno organizzate visite guidate a cura dell'associazione Amici dei Musei siciliani. Fra gli edifici aperti, c'è palazzo Chiaramente (lo Steri), in piazza Marina, in cui è esposta *La Vucciria* di Renato Guttuso, che, dipinta nel 1974, è stata donata dallo stesso artista all'Università di Palermo.

Kals'art cinema

MUSICA PER GLI OCCHI
Rassegna di Film-Concerto
A cura di Mario Bellone, Franco Marineo, Eric Biagi
atrio di palazzo Bonagia, inizio spettacoli ore 21,00
Produzione horns production

La manifestazione, finestra aperta su cinema, arti visive e musica, vuole rendere omaggio alla pratica della musicazione "live" di pellicole d'epoca. Musiche originali, cioè composte per l'occasione da qualificati musicisti siciliani, accompagneranno la proiezione di capolavori del cinema delle origini, in particolare del

xx

agency/design studio	client	art director	
Studio Priori & C. di Priori Roberto ss	Girasole	Roberto Priori	
×	× ×	× ×	×
×	× ×	× ×	×
designer	year	×	×
Roberto Priori	2005		
×	× ×	× ×	×
×	× ×	× ×	×

>089<

××

agency/design studio		client		art directors	
R&MAG		OutletSpace		Raffaele Fontanella	
				Maurizio Di Somma	
×	×	×	×	Marcello Cesar	×
×	×	×	×	×	×
designers		year			
Raffaele Fontanella		2006			
Maurizio Di Somma				×	×
Marcello Cesar	×	×	×	×	×
×	×	×	×	×	×

❯090❮

×××

agency/design studio	client	art director
Raineri design	Kome	William Raineri

× × × × × ×

× × × × ×

designer	year		
William Raineri	2005		

× ×

× × × × ×

× × × × × ×

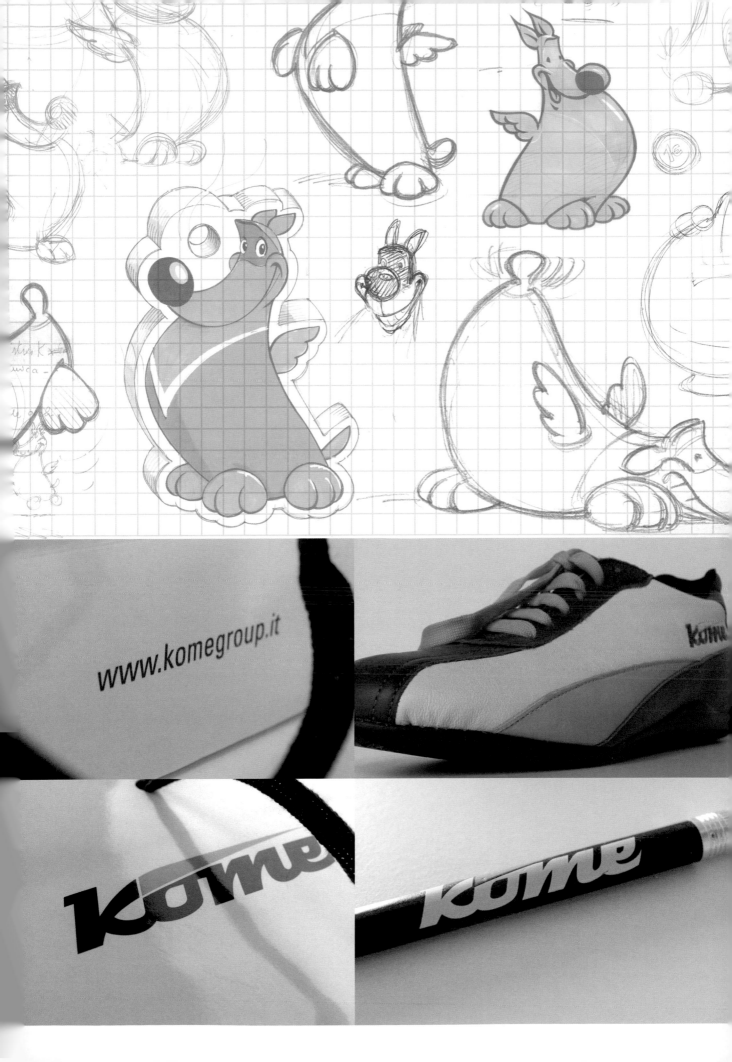

××

agency/design studio	client	art director
Raineri design	Possi gelatieri	William Raineri

× ×× × × ×

× × ×× × ×
designer × ×× × × ×
William Raineri 2007 ×

× ×× × × ×

× ×× × × ×

xxxxxxxxxxxxxxxxxxxxxxxxxxxxxxxxxxxxxxxxxxxxxxxxxxxxxxxxxxxxxxxxxxxxxxxxxxxxx

agency/design studio	client	art director
Zetalab	Moleskine	Lucio LuZo Lazzara

designers	year
Lucio LuZo Lazzara	2007
Stefano Lionetti	

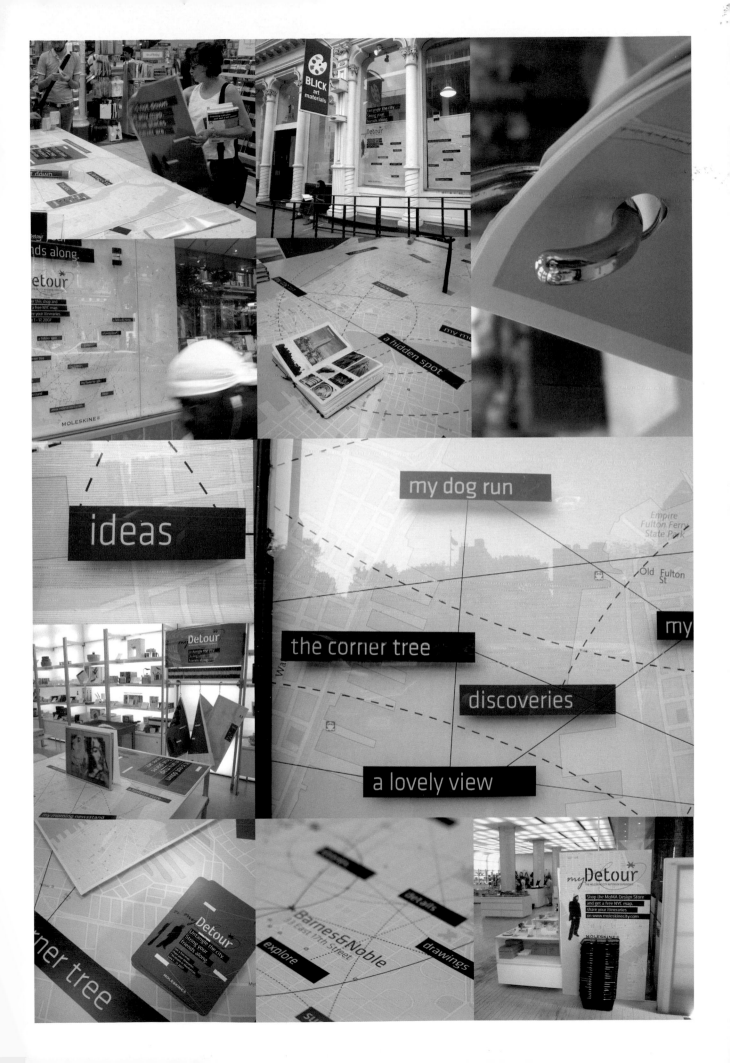

×××

agency/design studio	client	art director
Raineri design	Ken Barrell	William Raineri

× × × × × ×

× × × × ×

designer	year	
William Raineri	2006	

× ×

× × × × ×

× × × × ×

abcde
abcdefghijlmnopqrstuvwxyz

abcde
abcdefghijlmnopqrstuvwxyz

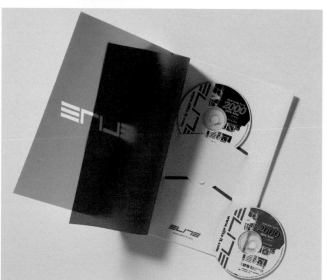

×××

agency/design studio	client	art director
Basso grafica e design	**Elite**	**Giuliano Basso**

×   ×   ×   ×   ×   ×

×   ×   ×   ×   ×

designer	year	
Giovanni Basso	**2002/2008**	

×   ×   ×   ×   ×   ×

×   ×   ×   ×   ×   ×

agency/design studio		client		art director		
Basso grafica e design		Elite		Giuliano Basso		
×	×	×		×	×	×
×	×	×		×	×	×
designer		year				
Giovanni Basso		2006			×	×
×	×	×		×	×	×
×	×	×		×	×	×

>106◀
××

agency/design studio	client	art director
Basso grafica e design	Set-up	Giuliano Basso

designer	year
Giovanni Basso	2005

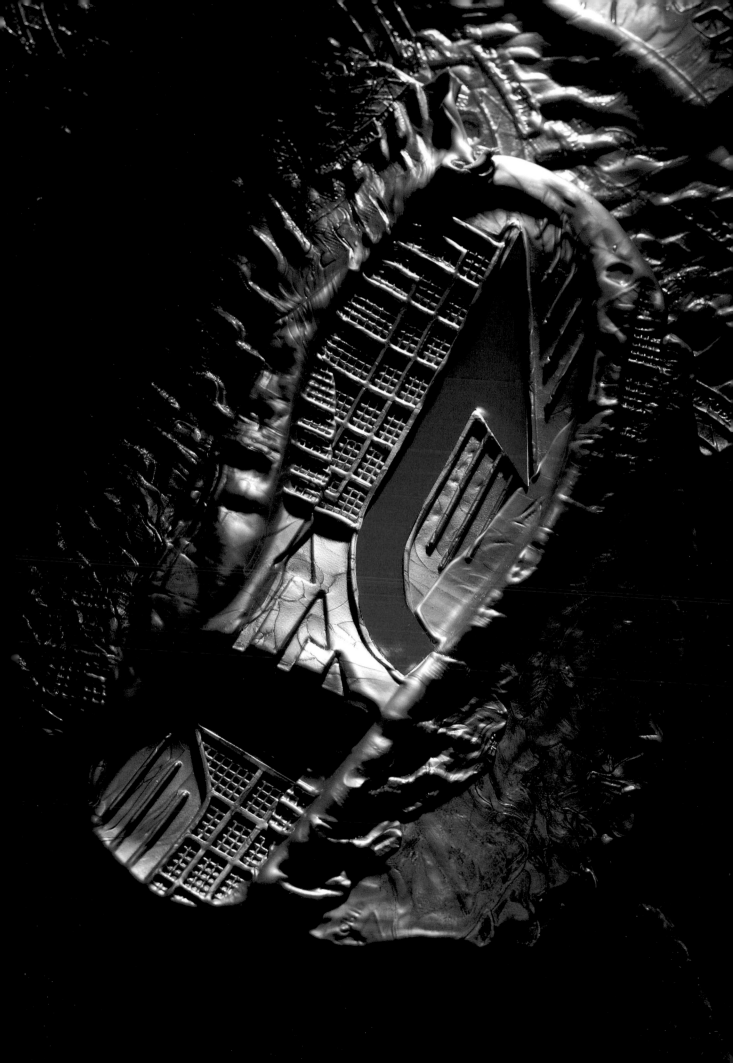

108

agency/design studio	client	art dircctor
Basso grafica e design	Ozone	Giuliano Basso

designer	year
Giovanni Basso	2005-2006

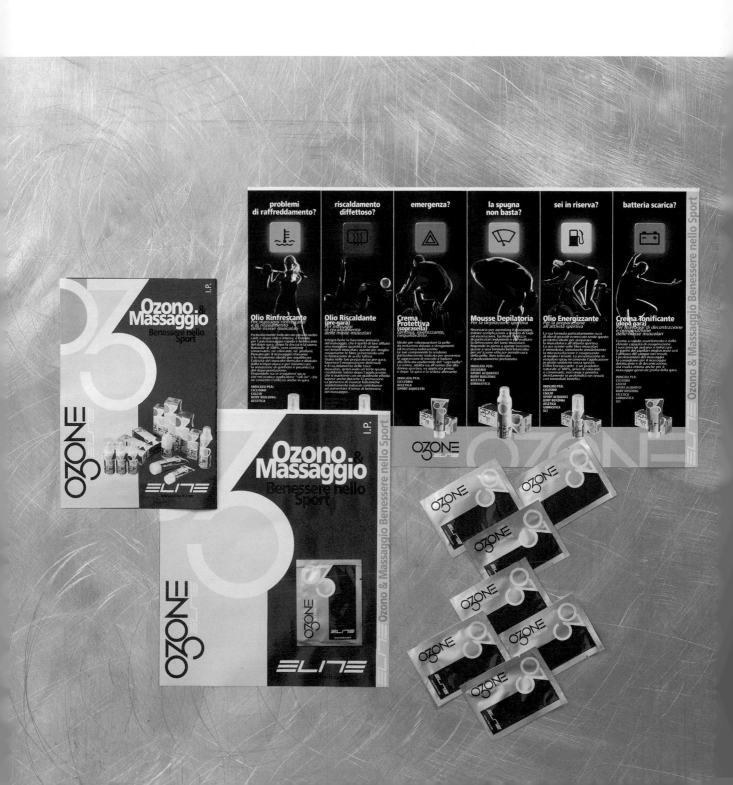

×××

agency/design studio		client		art director	
Basso grafica e design		Scilm		Giuliano Basso	
×	×	×		×	×
×	×	×		×	×
designer		year			
Giovanni Basso		1998/2006			
				×	×
×	×	×		×	×
×	×	×		×	×

carico
e scarico
merci

goods load
and unload

xxx

agency/design studio	client	art directors
Studio Kmzero	Dada/Hit of the Week	Francesco Canovaro Cosimo Lorenzo Pancini

Hit of the Week

designers	year
Francesco Canovaro Cosimo Lorenzo Pancini	2004

Hit of the Week

××

agency/design studio	client	art director	
Studio Kmzero	**Menta Fredda**	**Debora Manetti**	
×	× ×	× ×	×
×	× ×	× ×	×
designer	year	×	×
Debora Manetti	**2007**		
×	× ×	× ×	×

www.mentafredda.it

xxx

agency/design studio	client	art director
Temecula design	**Impasse**	**Cristiano de Veroli**

designer	year
Cristiano de Veroli	**2007**

HINDSIGHT
revolution.zine

agency/design studio	client	art director
Temecula design	Hindsight	Cristiano de Veroli

designer	year
Cristiano de Veroli	2007

×××

agency/design studio   client   art directors
Studio Kmzero   Lucca Comics & Games   Francesco Canovaro
                                                         Debora Manetti
×   ×   ×   × Cosimo Lorenzo Pancini   ×

×   ×   ×   × ×   ×
designers   year
Francesco Canovaro   2004/2005   ×
Debora Manetti
Cosimo Lorenzo Pancini ×   ×   × ×

×××

agency/design studio	client	art directors
Studio Kmzero	Studio Kmzero	Francesco Canovaro Debora Manetti Cosimo Lorenzo Pancini

designers	year
Francesco Canovaro Debora Manetti Cosimo Lorenzo Pancini	2007

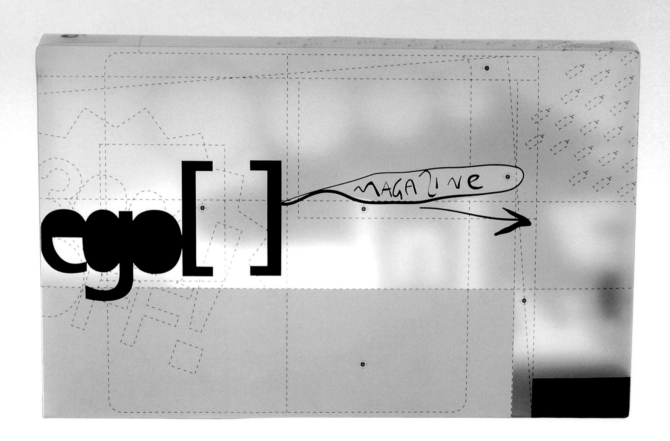

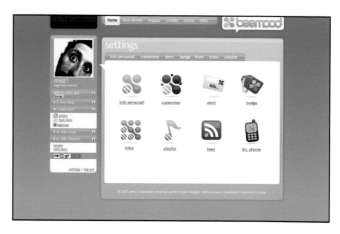

×××

agency/design studio		client		art director	
Studio Kmzero		Zero9 / BeeMood		Francesco Canovaro	
×	×	×	×	×	×
×	×	×	×	×	×
designer		year			
Francesco Canovaro		2007		×	×
×	×	×	×	×	×
×	×	×	×	×	×

xxxxxxxxxxxxxxxxxxxxxxxxxxxxxxxxxxxxxxxxxxxxxxxxxxxxxxxxxxxxxxxxxxxxxxxxx

agency/design studio		client		art directors	
Studio Kmzero		Comune di Firenze		Francesco Canovaro Cosimo Lorenzo Pancini	
×	×	×	×	×	×
×	×	×	×	×	×
designers		year			
Francesco Canovaro Cosimo Lorenzo Pancini		2007		×	×
×	×	×	×	×	×
×	×	×	×	×	×

××

agency/design studio	client	art director
Studio Kmzero	Appennino Riders	Francesco Canovaro

designer	year
Francesco Canovaro	2007

××

agency/design studio	client	art director
Studio Kmzero	**Aivy / Pink**	**Debora Manetti**

×   ×   ×   ×   ×   ×

designer	year
Debora Manetti	**2007**

mod. Tumarsky

xxx

agency/design studio	client	art director
Krghettojuice	Basic - London	Giovanni Paletta

×   ×   ×   ×   ×   ×

×   ×   ×   ×   ×   ×

designer	year
Giovanni Paletta	2006

×   ×   ×   ×

×   ×   ×   ×   ×   ×

×   ×   ×   ×   ×   ×

agency/design studio	client	art director
Alexander Egger	Arm The Lonely Records	Alexander Egger

× × × × × ×

× × × × ×

designer	year	
Alexander Egger	2007	

× × × × × ×

× × × × × ×

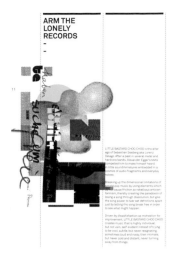

LITTLE BASTARD CHOO CHOO is the alter
ego of Sebastian Selzberg aka Lorenz
Delago. After a past in several metal and
hardcore bands, Alexander Egger's texts
compelled him to make himself heard
in little soundminiatures embedded in a
cosmos of audio fragments and everyday
noises.

Breaking up the dimensional limitations of
typical pop music by using elements which
would cause friction as rebellious anticon-
formism, thereby creating the paradoxon of
losing a song through dissolution, but give
the song power to tear set definitions apart
just by letting the song break free in order
to see what might happen.

Driven by dissatisfaction as motivation for
improvement, LITTLE BASTARD CHOO CHOO
creates music that is highly individual,
but not vain, self-evident instead of trying
to be cool, subtle but never resignating,
sometimes loud and noisy, then intimate,
but never cold and distant, never turning
away from things.

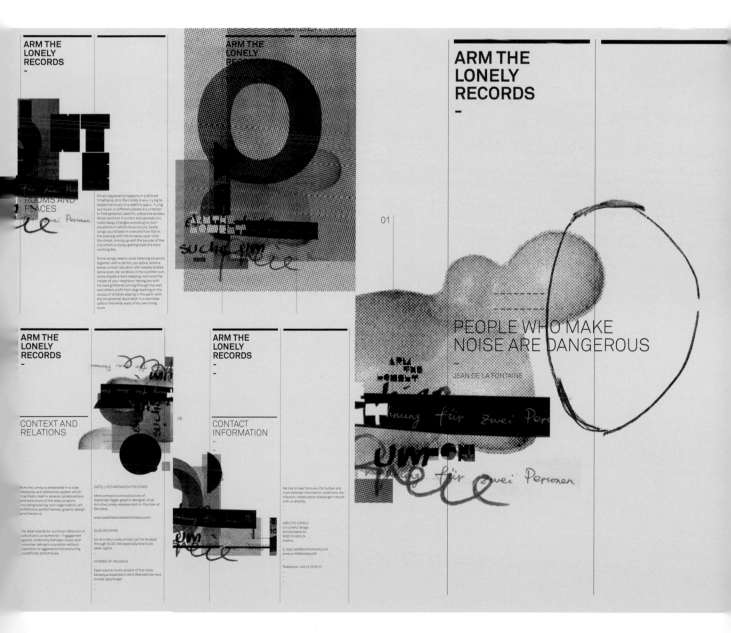

Music necessarily happens in a defined
timeframe. Arm the Lonely is also trying to
locate the music in a specific space. Trying
out music in different places is a criterion
to find personal, specific, subjective access.
Music anchors in a room and spreads out,
melts away, changes according to room
situations in which music occurs. Some
songs sound best in a second floor flat in
the evening with the windows open onto
the street, mixing up with the sounds of the
city which is slowly getting tired of a hard
working day.

Some songs need a close listening situation
together with a person you adore, some a
tense concert situation with sweaty bodies,
some open car windows in the summer sun,
some maybe a dark sleeping room and the
noises of your neighbour having sex with
his new girlfriend coming through the wall
and others profit from dogs barking or the
voices of children playing in the park, with
the ornamental decoration in a viennese
café or the white walls of my own living
room.

ROOMS AND
PLACES

01

PEOPLE WHO MAKE
NOISE ARE DANGEROUS

— JEAN DE LA FONTAINE

CONTEXT AND
RELATIONS

08

CONTACT
INFORMATION

Arm the Lonely is embedded in a wide
relational and referential system which
manifests itself in several collaborations
and extentions of the label program
including booking, tour organisation, art
exhibitions, performances, graphic design
and literature.

The label stands for a critical reflection of
culture and consumerism. Engagement
against conformity between music and
consumer taking in a position without
opposition or aggression but procuring
possibilities and choices.

SATELLITES MISTAKEN FOR STARS

More emissions and pollutions of
Alexander Egger, graphic designer of all
Arm the Lonely releases and co-founder of
the label.

www.satellitesmistakenforstars.com

DLGO BOOKING

All Arm the Lonely artists can be booked
through DLGO. We especially love to do
label nights.

HORSES OF CALIGULA

Open source music project of full-time
barbeque superstars Gerd Oberlechner and
Arnold Spachinger.

We like to hear from you. For further and
more detailed information, conditions, dis-
tribution, collaboration please get in touch
with us directly.

ARM THE LONELY
c/o Lorenz Delago
Amraborstrasse 44
6020 Innsbruck
Austria

E-mail: ask@armthelonely.com
www.armthelonely.com

Telephone: +43 23 35 60 01

ARM
THE
LONELY

------- ---

what you don't
understand
can mean anything

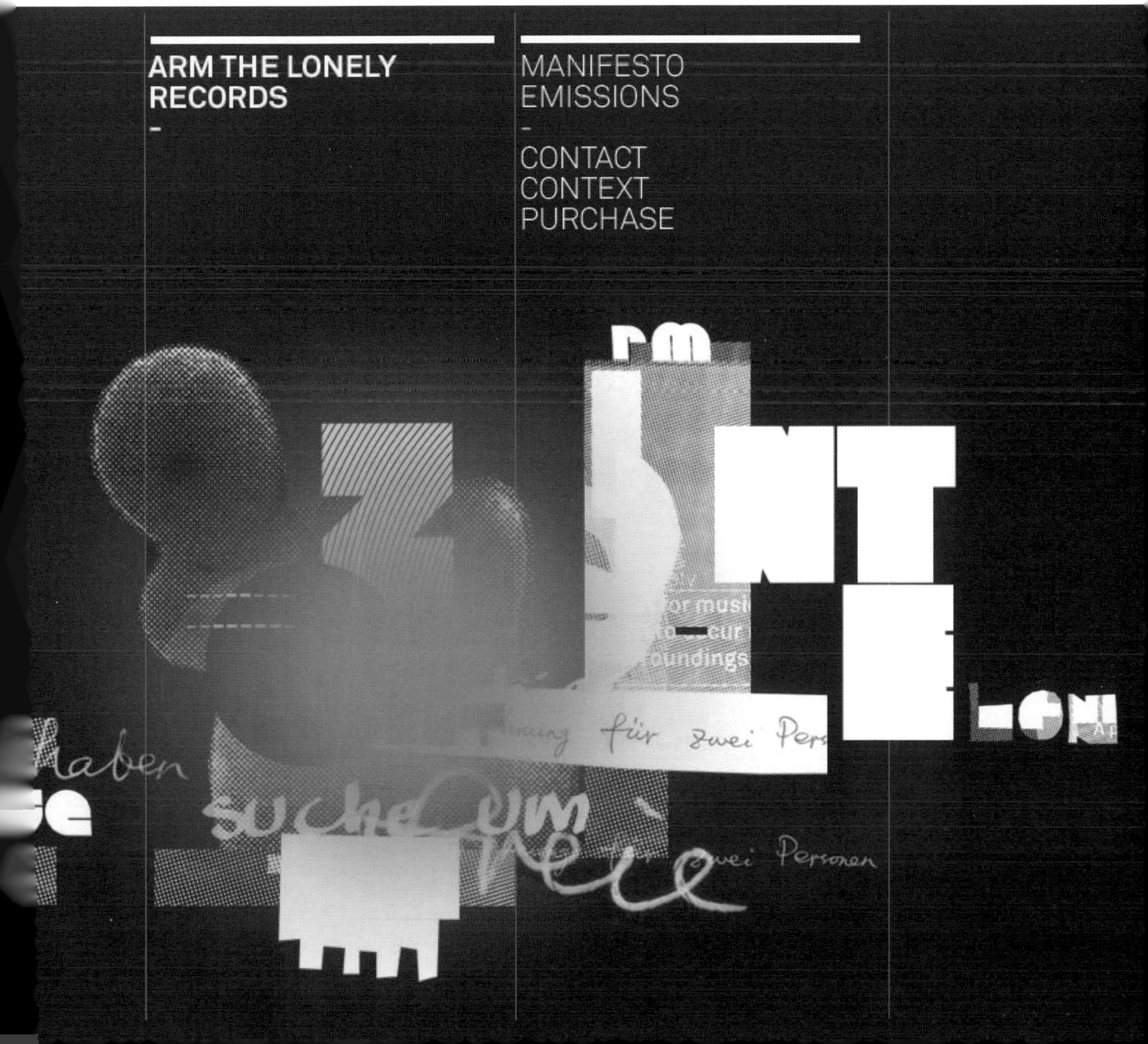

**ARM THE LONELY
RECORDS**

-

MANIFESTO
EMISSIONS

-

CONTACT
CONTEXT
PURCHASE

**Mood/
First Release Ever.**

agency/design studio	client	art director
Krghettojuice	Mood	Giovanni Paletta

designer	year
Giovanni Paletta	2005

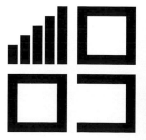

××

agency/design studio	client	art director
Krghettojuico	Coupè	Giovanni Paletta

designer	year
Giovanni Paletta	2006

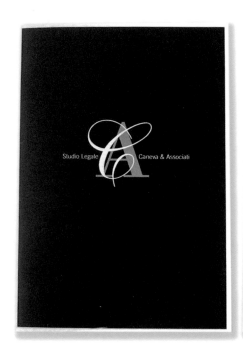

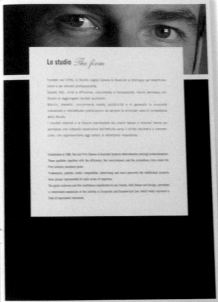

>132<

××

agency/design studio	client	art director
La Ditta Srl	Caneva e Associati	Scalzi Silvia

× × × × ×

× × × × ×

designer	year	×
Scalzi Silvia	2006	×

× × × × ×

× × × × ×

×××

agency/design studio		client		art director	
La Ditta Srl		**Studio di architettura A-side**		**Scalzi Silvia**	
×	×	×	×	×	×
×	×	×	×	×	×
designer		year			
Scalzi Silvia		**2007**		×	×
×	×	×	×	×	×
×	×	×	×	×	×

×××

agency/design studio		client		art director	
La Ditta Srl		**Azienda Agricola Agrivip**		**Scalzi Silvia**	
×	×	×	×	×	×
	×	×	×	×	×
designer		year			
Scalzi Silvia		**2006**			
				×	×
×	×	×	×	×	×
×	×	×	×	×	×

××

agency/design studio	client	art director	
La Ditta Srl	Avvocato Elena Carpani	Scalzi Silvia	
×	×	×	×
×	×	×	×
designer	year	×	×
Scalzi Silvia	2006	×	×
×	×	×	×
×	×	×	×

xxx

agency/design studio	client	art director
Leandro Mastria Design **Pitagora Comunicazione**	**Treviso Servizi**	**Leandro Mastria**

designer	year
Pitagora Creative Division	**2006**

xxx

agency/design studio	client	art director
Aspirine	Aspirine	Gian Pietro Farinelli

designer	year
Gian Pietro Farinelli	2004

xx

agency/design studio	client	art director
Basso grafica e design	**Officio**	**Giuliano Basso**

designer	year
Giovanni Basso	**2003**

I CORTILI DEI MASI*
SAN GIACOMO

SAN GIACOMO*
BUILDINGS

SAN GIACOMO COSTRUZIONI srl
P.IVA e C.F. 01 695 160 380
Sede Legale Via Borgoleoni. 63
Uff. Comm. Via Armari. 28 . 44100 Ferrara . IT
Ph. +39 0532 20 71 08   F. +39 0532 24 01 30
site . sangiacomo.biz   email . info@sangiacomo.biz

SAN GIACOMO*
BUILDINGS

SAN GIACOMO*
BUILDINGS

SAN GIACOMO COSTRUZIONI srl
P.IVA e C.F. 01 695 160 380
Sede Legale Via Borgoleoni. 63
Uffici Commerciali Via Armari. 28 . 44100 Ferrara . IT
Ph. +39 0532 20 71 08   F. +39 0532 24 01 30
site . sangiacomo.biz   email . info@sangiacomo.biz

I CORTILI DEI MASI
SAN GIACOMO

SAN GIACOMO*
BUILDINGS

>140<
×××

agency/design studio	client	art director
Aspirine	**San Giacomo Costruzioni**	**Gian Pietro Farinelli**

designer	year
Gian Pietro Farinelli	**2007**

Il grande dono dei designer è quello di dare un'anima a oggetti che di per sé sarebbero solo utili. Professionisti con una formazione tecnica unita a un senso artistico ed estetico. Ed è anche per loro che nasce SEDICI. Un'area nuova, dove con magistrale sapienza, si è recuperata l'archeologia industriale preesistente per trasformarla in un quartiere all'avanguardia dove tutti i professionisti della creatività troveranno un habitat ideale per lavorare e creare. Qui i designer troveranno stimoli culturali, persone con cui scambiare opinioni su tematiche attuali, ampi spazi da cui trarre ispirazione per le nuove creazioni e un'atmosfera ideale per chi ha come obiettivo nella vita la progettazione ∎

eclettico

«L'osservazione della realtà è uno stimolo continuo per dare volume a idee sempre nuove»

xxxxxxxxxxxxxxxxxxxxxxxxxxxxxxxxxxxxxxxxxxxxxxxxxxxxxxxxxxxxxxxxxxxxxxxxxxx

agency/design studio		client		art directors	
Attus&Scarfone		**Pirelli Re**		**Ettore Scarfone** **Andrea Attus**	
x	x	x		x	x
			x	x	
designers	x	year	x	x	x
Ettore Scarfone **Andrea Attus**		**2006**		x	x
x	x	x		x	x
x	x	x	x	x	x

xxxxxxxxxxxxxxxxxxxxxxxxxxxxxxxxxxxxxxxxxxxxxxxxxxxxxxxxxxxxxxxxxxxxxxxxxxxxxxxxxxxxxxxxxxxxxxxxxx

agency/design studio	client	art director
Oikos Associati sas	Oikos Associati sas	Isabella Garlati

designer	year
Isabella Garlati	2003

xx

agency/design studio	client	art director
Oikos Associati sas	Biancheruss srl	Isabella Garlati

× × × × ×

× × × × ×

designer	year		
Isabella Garlati	2005	×	×

× × × × ×

× × × × ×

×××

agency/design studio	client	art director
Bonacini Idea di Osvaldo Bonacini	**Shibuya**	**Lorenza Zanni**

designer	year
Lorenza Zanni	**2007**

×××

agency/design studio	client	art directors	
Cacao Design	Ka-Kao Fusion restaurant	Mauro Pastore Masa Magnoni Alessandro Floridia	
×	×	×	×
		×	×
designers	year		
Alessandro Floridia Giulia Landini	2006		
		×	×
×	×	×	×
×	×	× ×	×

×××

agency/design studio	client	art director	
Insidebtb	**Malua SRL**	**Luca Targa**	
×	× ×	× ×	×
×	× ×	× ×	×
designer	year		
Luca Targa	**2006**	×	×
×	× ×	× ×	×
×	× ×	˅ ˅	ǝ

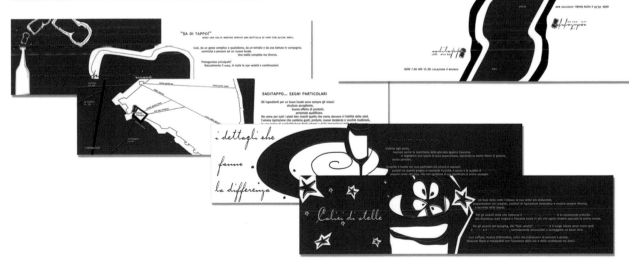

×××

agency/design studio		client		art director	
Alexander Egger		Acherer		Alexander Egger	
×	×	×	×	×	×
×	×	×	×	×	×
designer		year			×
Alexander Egger		2007			×
×	×	×		×	×
×	×	×		×	×

×××

agency/design studio	client	art director
abc&z	Gelateria "Cremeria Funivia"	Matteo Carboni

× × × × ×

× × × × ×

designer	year
Matteo Carboni	2006

× ×

× × × × ×

× × × × ×

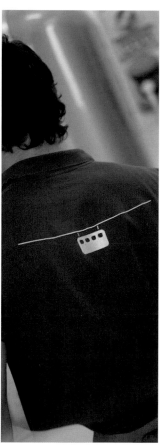

agency/design studio		client		art director		
Alexander Egger		Acherer		Alexander Egger		
×	×	×		×	×	×
×	×	×		×	×	×
designer		year			×	×
Alexander Egger		2007				
×	×	×		×	×	×
×	×	×		×	×	×

KATHARINA ENTLER

GESCHÄFTSFÜHRERIN

DAS COMPTOIR, Waldandachtstraße 2, 2540 Bad Vöslau
T +43 2252 72 773 40, F +43 2252 72 773 72
M +43 664 150 60 46, dascomptoir@dascomptoir.at
www.dascomptoir.at

SCHAURAUM

DAS COMPTOIR, Waldandachtstraße 2, 2540 Bad Vöslau
T +43 2252 72 773 40, F +43 2252 72 773 72
dascomptoir@dascomptoir.at, www.dascomptoir.at

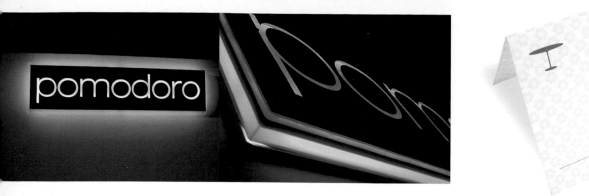

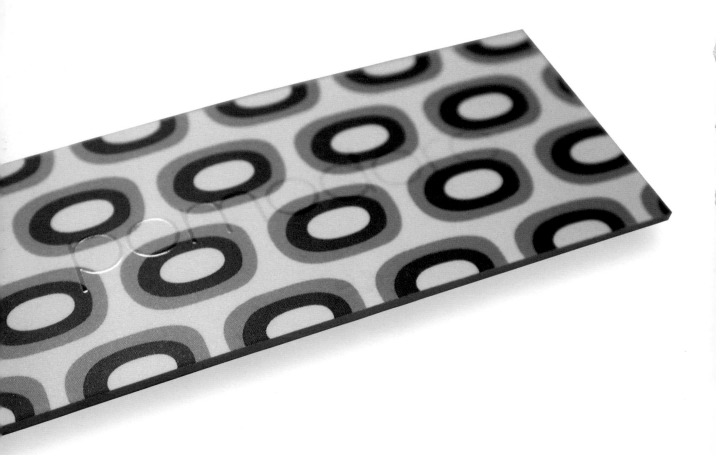

×××

agency/design studio	client	art director
Aspirine	**Pomodoro**	**Gian Pietro Farinelli**

designer	year
Gian Pietro Farinelli	**2002/2003**

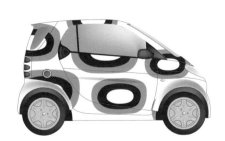

Art Center College Library
1700 Lida Street
Pasadena, CA 91103

xxxxxxxxxxxxxxxxxxxxxxxxxxxxxxxxxxxxxxxxxxxxxxxxxxxxxxxxxxxxxxxxxxxxxxxxxxxxxxxxxxxxxxxxxxx

agency/design studio		client		art director		
Matitegiovanotte		**Proeco**		**Giovanni Pizzigati**		
x	x	x		x		x
x	x	x		x		x
designers		year				x
Giovanni Pizzigati		**2006/2007**				x
Barbara Longiardi						
Alessandro Maltoni	x	x		x	x	x
x	x	x		x	x	x

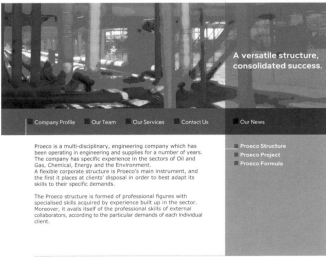

PROECO
Future Under Construction

ITA | ENG

A versatile structure, consolidated success.

Company Profile · Our Team · Our Services · Contact Us · Our News

Proeco is a multi-disciplinary, engineering company which has been operating in engineering and supplies for a number of years. The company has specific experience in the sectors of Oil and Gas, Chemical, Energy and the Environment.
A flexible corporate structure is Proeco's main instrument, and the first it places at clients' disposal in order to best adapt its skills to their specific demands.

The Proeco structure is formed of professional figures with specialised skills acquired by experience built up in the sector. Moreover, it avails itself of the professional skills of external collaborators, according to the particular demands of each individual client.

- Proeco Structure
- Proeco Project
- Proeco Formula

Copyright 2007 Proeco Srl ® - Privacy Policy

×××

agency/design studio			client		art director	
Studio Sancisi			**Unitycoop**		**Nicola Sancisi**	
			Social Business Community			
×	×	×		×	×	×
×		×	×	×	×	×
designer			year			
Nicola Sancisi			**2007**			
					×	×
×	×	×	×	×	×	
×		×	×		×	×

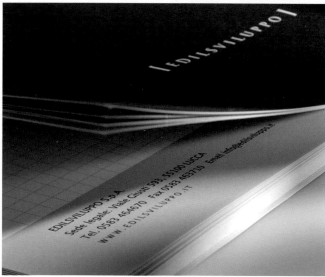

×××

agency/design studio	client	art director
Lindbergh Comunicazione	Edilsviluppo	Luca Giorgi

×	×	×	×

designer	year
Caroline Georget	2006

[EDILSVILUPPO]
ABITARE LA QUALITÀ

GRAND HOTEL
PRINCIPE DI PIEMONTE
★ ★ ★ ★
LUXURY

×××

agency/design studio	client	art director
Lindbergh Comunicazione	Principe di Piemonte	Luca Giorgi

designer	year
Caroline Georget	2007

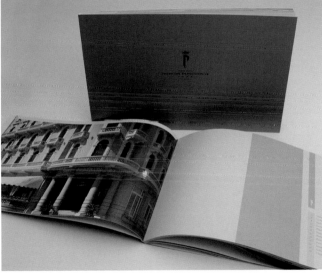

×××

agency/design studio	client	art director
Lindbergh Comunicazione	**Rontani**	**Luca Giorgi**

×   ×   ×   ×   ×   ×

designer	year	
Caroline Georget	**2007**	

×   ×   ×   ×   ×

×   ×   ×   ×   ×

×××

agency/design studio	client	art director
Linke	Linke srl Advergame	Rossella Lezzi

designer	year
Rossella Lezzi	2006

>162<

xxxxxxxxxxxxxxxxxxxxxxxxxxxxxxxxxxxxxxxxxxxxxxxxxxxxxxxxxxxxxxxxxxxxxx

agency/design studio	client	art director	
Linke	Linke srl	Rossella Lezzi	
×	×	×	×
×	×	×	×
designer	year		
Rossella Lezzi	2005		
		×	×
×	×	×	×
×	×	×	×

××

agency/design studio	client	art director
Linke	Kókos onlus	Rossella Lezzi

designer	year
Rossella Lezzi	2005

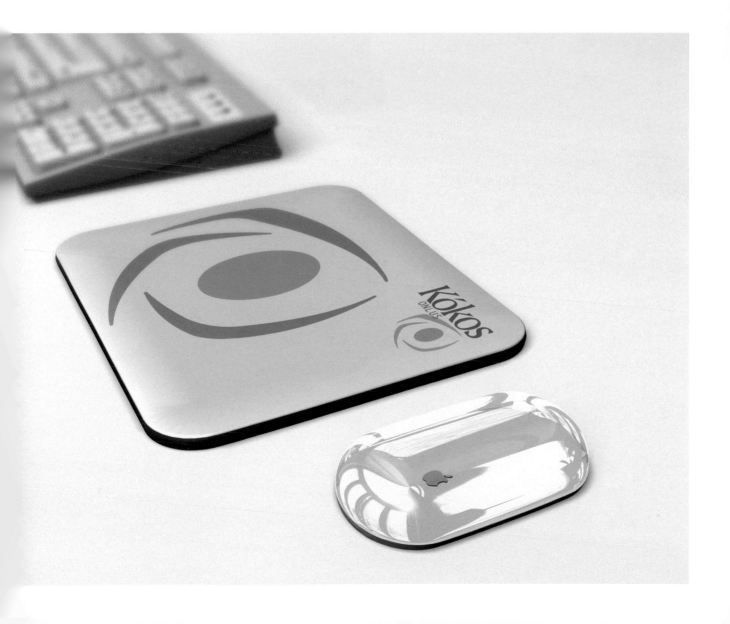

agency/design studio	client	art director	
Linke	Magris S.p.A	Rossella Lezzi	
designer	year		
Rossella Lezzi	2004/2007		

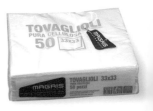

agency/design studio	client	art director
Linke	Zupperman	Rossella Lezzi

designer	year
Rossella Lezzi	2005

×××

agency/design studio	client	creative director
Admcom	Admcom	Maurizio Cinti

designer/art director	copywriters	year
Manuel dall'Olio	Silva Fedrigo Massimiliano Pancaldi	2008

×××

agency/design studio
Matitegiovanotte

client
Tiziana

art directors
Antonella Bandoli
Barbara Longiardi

designer
Barbara Longiardi

year
2007

agency/design studio	client	art directors
Matitegiovanotte	**Stone**	**Giovanni Pizzigati**
		Antonella Bandoli

designer	year
Giovanni Pizzigati	**2004**

×××

agency/design studio	client	art directors	
Cacao Design	Kiver	Mauro Pastore	
		Masa Magnoni	
×	× ×	Alessandro Floridia ×	×
×	× ×	× ×	×
designer	year	×	×
Creative team	2005		
×	× ×	× ×	×
×	× ×	× ×	×

xx

agency/design studio	client	art directors	
Cacao Design	Output	Mauro Pastore	
		Masa Magnoni	
		Alessandro Floridia	

designer	year		
Luisa Piras	2005		

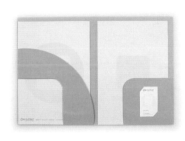

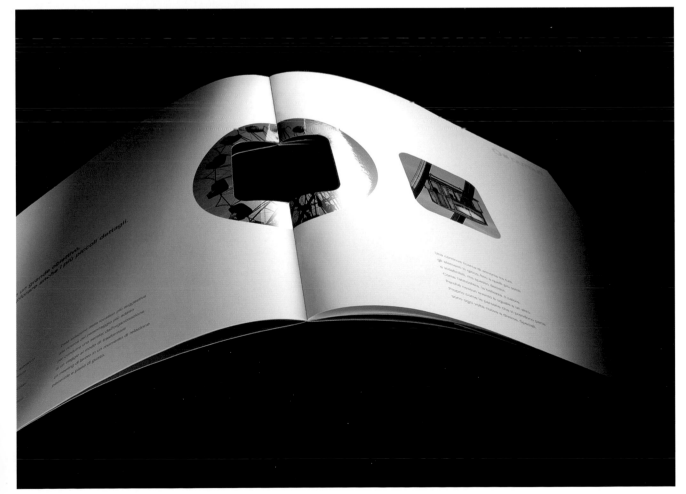

agency/design studio	client	art director	
Alexander Egger	Red-Hot	Alexander Egger	
×	× ×	× ×	×
×	× ×	× ×	×
designer	year	×	×
Alexander Egger	2007	×	
×	× ×	× ×	×
×	× ×	× ×	×

tel +43 1 533 30 34-25
fax +43 1 533 30 34-28
office@red-hot.com

red-hot

short facts
biography

hard facts
secrets of the trade

portfolio
red-hot solution
red-hot communication
red-hot surprise
red-hot consulting
red-hot celebration

schmalzhofgasse 8/16
1060 vienna/austria

clients
promotion
events
marketing
list

partner

contact

---

hard facts

weiter
zurück

**red-hot – das brandaktuelle Projekt, das aus einer lange
gehorteten, wohl überlegten, immer wieder durchdachten Idee
in die Wirklichkeit umgesetzt wurde.**

Wir stehen Ihnen als auf den ersten Blick kleine, dadurch auch
äußerst flexible und gerade deswegen kompetente Berater im
Marketingbereich mit unterschiedlichen Schwerpunkten rund
um die Uhr zur Verfügung. Wer einen Blick hinter unsere Kulissen
wirft, dem offenbart sich unser umfassendes Netzwerk an
Kontakten in die Kreativ-, Künstler- und Eventszene, das Ihnen
die passende, gerne auch außergewöhnliche Umsetzung all Ihrer
konkreten Wünsche und halbkonkreten Ideen für Ihre
Unternehmenskommunikation garantiert. Von der Erst- oder
Neugestaltung Ihres Webauftrittes, über PR-Maßnahmen unter
Nutzung unserer umfassenden Mailverteiler bis hin zu
überraschenden Guerilla Marketing Aktivitäten – zu jeder
tages- und nachtzeit beraten wir Sie gerne und setzen dann die
maßgeschneiderten Lösungen in die Tat um.

we collaborate
with top designers

---

tel +43 1 533 30 34-25
fax +43 1 533 30 34-28
office@red-hot.com

RED-HOT

short facts
biography

hard facts
secrets of the trade

portfolio
red-hot solution
red-hot communication
red-hot surprise
red-hot consulting
red-hot celebration

schmalzhofgasse 8/16
1060 vienna/austria

clients
promotion
events
marketing
list

partner

contact

---

solution

weiter
zurück

Von der Status-quo Analyse ihrer momentanen Website bis hin
zur Integration eines passenden Content Management Systems
(CMS) und dem Re-Design Ihrer digitalen Corporate Identity (CI),
nehmen wir uns allen digitalen Bedürfnissen an und überraschen
Sie mit der Lösung, nach der Sie immer gesucht haben

---

tel +43 1 533 30 34–25
fax +43 1 533 30 34–28

r

with
compliments

schmalzhofgasse 8/16
1060 vienna/austria

www.red-hot.com
office@red-hot.com

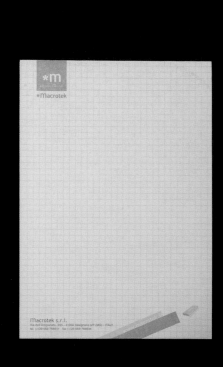

××

agency/design studio		client		art director	
Cosmographix		Macrotek		Alberto Baracchi	
×	×	×	×	×	×
designer	×	year	×	×	×
Alberto Baracchi		2007		×	×
×	×	×	×	×	×
×	×	×	×	×	×

*macrotek

G/ LLERI/ D'/ RTE MODERN/ P/ LERMO

xxxxxxxxxxxxxxxxxxxxxxxxxxxxxxxxxxxxxxxxxxxxxxxxxxxxxxxxxxxxxxxxxxxxxxxxxxxxxxx

agency/design studio	client	art director
Carré Noir	Galleria d'Arte Moderna di Palermo	Massimiliano Sagrati

x   x   x   x   x   x

x   x   x   x   x   x

designers	year	
Massimiliano Sagrati	2006	
Hanna Lehtinen		

x   x   x   x   x

x   x   x   x   x   x

xxx

agency/design studio	client	art director
Carré Noir	Ferrovie Nord Milano	Massimiliano Sagrati

designers	year
Massimiliano Sagrati	2006
Emanuela Cappelli	
Hanna Lehtinen	

xx

agency/design studio		client		art director		
Carré Noir		**FIAT**		**Enrico Maria Pecchio**		
×	×	×		×	×	×
	×	×		×		×
designer		year			×	×
Carré Noir		**2007**				
×	×	×		×	×	×
×	×	×		×	×	×

agency/design studio	client	art director
Carré Noir	Abarth	Enrico Maria Pecchio

designer	year
Carré Noir	2007

xx

agency/design studio		client		art director	
Cristiano Ambrosioni		MK Maki Eventi		Cristiano Ambrosioni	
×	×	×	×	×	×
×	×	×	×	×	×
designer		year		×	×
Cristiano Ambrosioni		2007		×	×
×	×	×	×	×	×
×	×	×	×	×	×

> 181 ◀
xxxxxxxxxxxxxxxxxxxxxxxxxxxxxxxxxxxxxxxxxxxxxxxxxxxxxxxxxxxxxxxx

agency/design studio		client		art director	
Cristiano Ambrosioni		**Bonate Costruzioni**		**Cristiano Ambrosioni**	
×	×	×	×	×	×
×	×	×	×	×	×
designer		year			×	×
Cristiano Ambrosioni		**2007**		×	×
×	×	×	×	×	×
×	×	×	×	×	×

BONATE COSTRUZIONI   BONATE COSTRUZIONI

> 182 <
xxxxxxxxxxxxxxxxxxxxxxxxxxxxxxxxxxxxxxxxxxxxxxxxxxxxxxxxxxxxxxxxxxxxxxxxxxxxx

agency/design studio		client		art director	
Cambiamenti		**La Credenza**		**Niels Guerrini**	
x	x	x	x	x	x
x	x	x	x	x	x
designers		year			
Laura Zavalloni		**2004**		x	x
Niels Guerrini					
x	x	x	x	x	x
x	x	x	x	x	x

×××

agency/design studio		client		art director	
Carré Noir		Autogrill		Enrico Maria Pecchio	
×	×	×	×	×	×
×	×	×	×	×	×
designer		year		×	×
Carré Noir		2007		×	×
×	×	×	×	×	×
×	×	×	×	×	×

××

agency/design studio		client		art directors	
Cambiamenti		**C'enoteca**		**Carlo Zauli** **Laura Zavalloni**	
×	×	×	×	×	×
×	×	×	×	×	×
designer		year			
Laura Zavalloni		**2005**		×	×
×	×	×	×	×	×
×	×	×	×	×	×

>185<

xxxxxxxxxxxxxxxxxxxxxxxxxxxxxxxxxxxxxxxxxxxxxxxxxxxxxxxxxxxxxxxxxxxxxxxxx

agency/design studio		client		art directors	
Cambiamenti		La Corte di Bacco		Carlo Zauli Alessandro Antonelli	
×	×	×	×	×	×
×	×	×	×	×	×
designer		year		×	×
Jan Guerrini		2004			
×	×	×	×	×	×
×	×	×	×	×	×

×××

agency/design studio		client		art directors	
Cacao Design		Fontegrafica		Mauro Pastore	
				Masa Magnoni	
×	×	×	×	Alessandro Floridia	×
×	×	×	×	×	×
designer		year			
Creative team		2005/2007		×	×
×	×	×	×	×	×
×	×	×	×	×	×

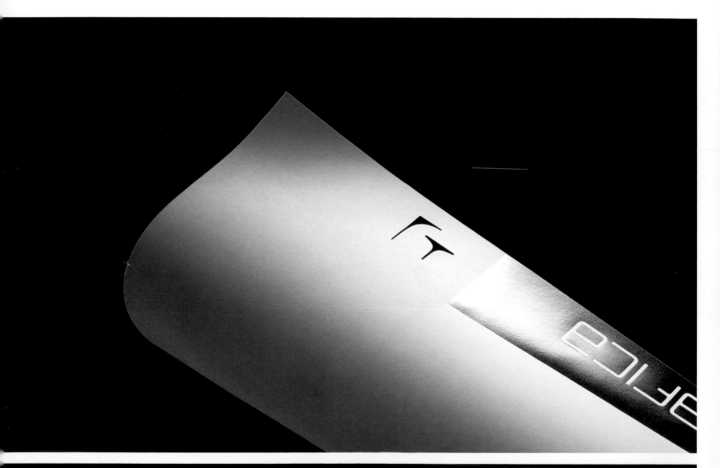

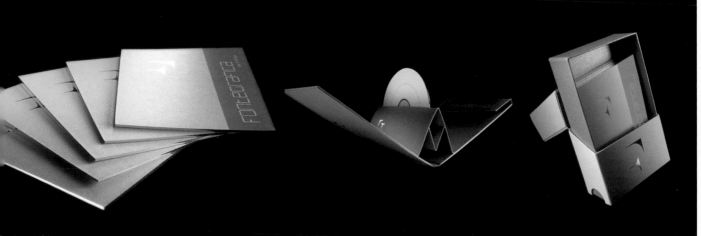

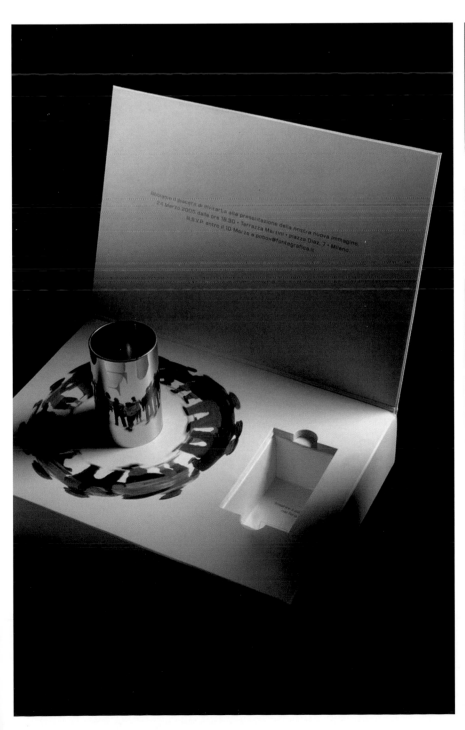

Ricevere il piacere di invitarla alla presentazione della nostra nuova immagine
24 Marzo 2005 dalle ore 18.30 • Terrazza Martini • piazza Diaz, 7 • Milano
R.S.V.P. entro il 10 Marzo a pobox@fontegrafica.it

×××

agency/design studio	client	art director	
Carré Noir	Finmeccanica	Massimiliano Sagrati	
×	×	×	×
×	×	×	×
designers	year	×	×
Massimiliano Sagrati	2006	×	×
Emanuela Cappelli			
Alfredo Laneve	×	×	×
Hanna Lehtinen			
×	×	×	×

×××

agency/design studio
Carré Noir

client
Johnson Wax

art director
Enrico Maria Pecchio

×   × ×   × ×   ×

×   × ×   × ×   ×

designer   year
Carré Noir   **2007**

×   × ×   × ×   ×

×   × ×   ×   ×

××

agency/design studio	client	art director
Studio Sancisi	**Location!Location!** **Servizi per eventi e media**	**Nicola Sancisi**
×	×	×
×	×	×
designer	year	
Nicola Sancisi	**2007**	
×	×	×
×	×	×

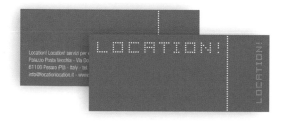

×××

agency/design studio	client	art director
Studio Sancisi	THW - Bundesanstalt Technisches Hilfswerk - Bonn	Nicola Sancisi

designer	year
Nicola Sancisi	2007

EU **EXCHANGE** OF **EXPERTS** IN CIVIL PROTECTION

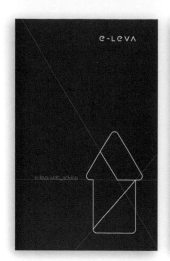

×××

agency/design studio	client	art director
Studio Sancisi	**E-leva srl**	**Nicola Sancisi**

×   × ×   × ×   ×

designer	year
Nicola Sancisi	**2004/2007**

××

| agency/design studio | client | art director |
| StudioGuida | Edizioni d'if | Francesco E. Guida |

×   ×   ×   ×   ×   ×

| designer | year |
| Francesco E. Guida | 2001/2007 |

×   ×

×   ×   ×   ×   ×   ×

×   ×   ×   ×   ×   ×

d'if

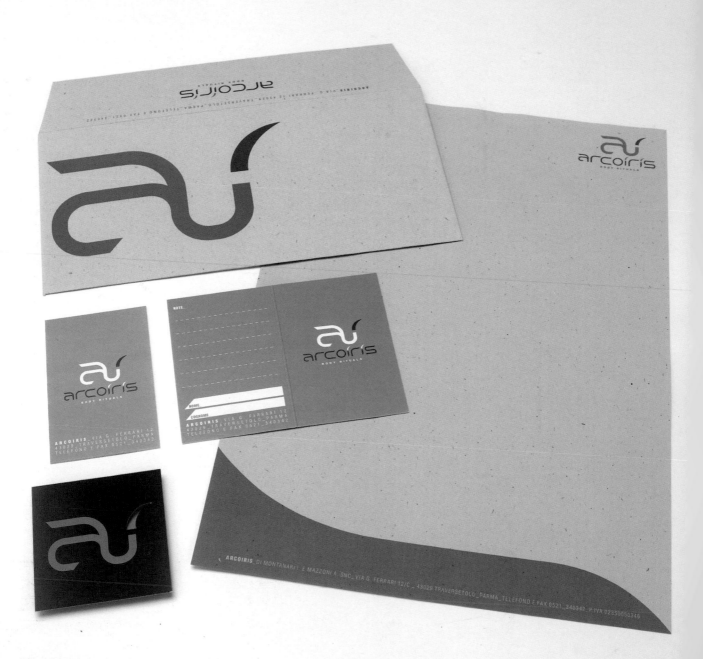

××

agency/design studio	client	art director
Kalimera	**Arcoiris**	**Kalimera**
×	×	×	×	×
×	×	×	×	×
designer	year	
Kalimera	**2006**	
×	×	×	×
×	×	×	×

agency/design studio	client	art director
Kalimera	Ceramiche Supergres	Kalimera

designer	year
Kalimera	2007

agency/design studio		client	art director	
Cambiamenti		Enò	Carlo Zauli	
×	×	×	×	×
×	×	×	× ×	×
designers		year		
Jan Guerrini		2003	×	×
Carlo Zauli				
×	×	×	× ×	×
×	×	×	× ×	×

××

agency/design studio	client	art director
Cambiamenti	Verdura	Carlo Zauli

× × × × ×

× × × × ×

designers	year
Jan Guerrini	2004
Laura Zavalloni	

× × × × × ×

× × × × × ×

xxxxxxxxxxxxxxxxxxxxxxxxxxxxxxxxxxxxxxxxxxxxxxxxxxxxxxxxxxxxxxxxxxxxxxxxx

agency/design studio	client	art director
Akuna Matata	**Akuna Matata**	**Giuseppe Lucchetti**

× × × × × × ×

× × × × × × ×

designer	year	
Giuseppe Lucchetti	**2007**	× ×

× × × × × ×

× × × × × × ×

200

agency/design studio	client	art director
Esseblu	Business Press	Susanna Vallebona

designer	year
Susanna Vallebona	2006

agency/design studio
Due mani non bastano

client
Naturello

art director
Davide Longaretti

✕   ✕ ✕   ✕ ✕   ✕

✕   ✕ ✕   ✕ ✕   ✕

designer
Ilaria Faccioli

year
2006/2007

                       ✕   ✕

✕   ✕ ✕   ✕ ✕   ✕

✕   ✕ ✕   ✕ ✕   ✕

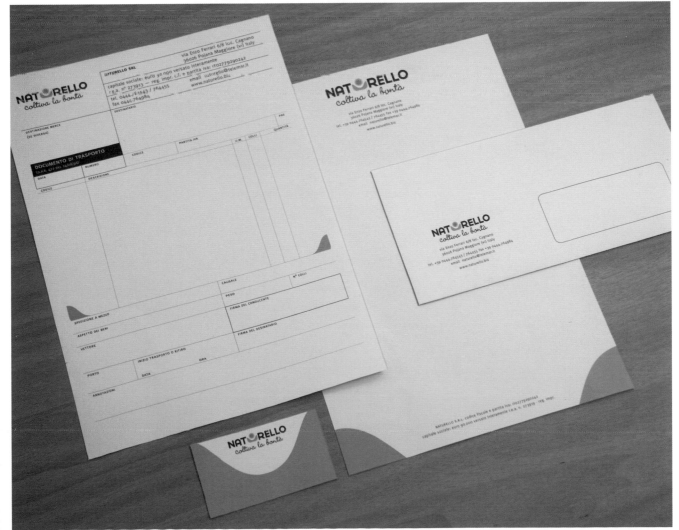

xxxxxxxxxxxxxxxxxxxxxxxxxxxxxxxxxxxxxxxxxxxxxxxxxxxxxxxxxxxxxxxxxxxxxxx

agency/design studio		client		art director	
Due mani non bastano		Terre di mezzo		Nicolò Bottarelli	
×	×	×	×	×	×
×	×	×	×	×	×
designer		year			
Ilaria Faccioli		2006			
×	×	×	×	×	×
×	×	×	×	×	×

xx

agency/design studio		client		art director	
Equilibrisospesi		Comune di Russi		Equilibrisospesi	
×	×	×	×	×	×
×	×	×	×	×	×
designer		year		×	×
Equilibrisospesi		2007		×	×
×	×	×	×	×	×
×	×	×	×	×	×

agency/design studio	client	art director
Equilibrisospesi	**Spirito Verde**	**Equilibrisospesi**

× × × × ×

designer	year			
Equilibrisospesi	**2007**			

× × × × ×

× × × × ×

×××

agency/design studio	client	art director
Doppiazeta	Claudio Cattani Training	Lorenza Zanni

designer	year	
Lorenza Zanni	2007	

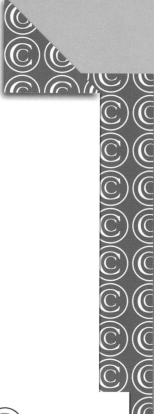

×××

agency/design studio	client	art director
Equilibrisospesi	Valtorto - Associazione Culturale	Equilibrisospesi

×   ×   ×   ×   ×   ×

×   ×   ×   ×   ×   ×

designer	year	
Equilibrisospesi	2006	

×   ×   ×

×   ×   ×   ×   ×   ×

×   ×   ×   ×   ×   ×

208

xxxxxxxxxxxxxxxxxxxxxxxxxxxxxxxxxxxxxxxxxxxxxxxxxxxxxxxxxxxxxxxxxxxxxxxxxxxxxxxx

agency/design studio	client	art director
Fachiro Strategic Design	Centro Servizi per il Volontariato Mantovano	Amedeo Palazzi

designer	year
Silvia Grisanti	2003/2007

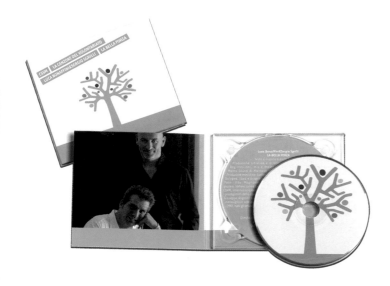

❯209❮

xxxxxxxxxxxxxxxxxxxxxxxxxxxxxxxxxxxxxxxxxxxxxxxxxxxxxxxxxxxxxxxx

agency/design studio	client	art director
Fachiro Strategic Design	Democratici di Sinistra	Amedeo Palazzi

designer	year
Amedeo Palazzi	2005

xx

agency/design studio	client	art director
Fachiro Strategic Design	**Comune di Mantova, Provincia di Mantova, ampe, silb, Prefettura di Mantova, Questura di Mantova**	**Amedeo Palazzi**

designer	year
Amedeo Palazzi	**2003/2005**

Ci rivediamo lunedì

xx

agency/design studio	client	art director
Fachiro Strategic Design	**Azienda corvizi alla persona e alla famiglia - Comune di Mantova**	**Amedeo Palazzi**

designer	year
Silvia Grisanti	**2005**

×××

agency/design studio	client	art director
Fachiro Strategic Design	**Fiera Millenaria di Gonzaga**	**Amedeo Palazzi**

designer	year
Silvia Grisanti	**2000/2007**

Fiera Millenaria di Gonzaga
1~9 settembre 2007
www.fieramillenaria.it

\ agricoltura \ zootecnia \ agroalimentare \ arte \ artigianato \ commercio \ cultura \ folklore \ gastronomia \ spettacoli

BAM Banca Agricola Mantovana
GRUPPO MPS

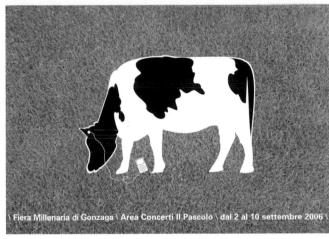

\ Fiera Millenaria di Gonzaga \ Area Concerti Il Pascolo \ dal 2 al 10 settembre 2006 \

>214<

×××

agency/design studio	client	art director
Dinamo Project	**Corretto Suite**	**Marco Bedeschi**

designers	year
Marco Bedeschi	**2007**
Michele Santandrea	

×××

agency/design studio		client		art director		
Dinamo Project		Kepos		Marco Bedeschi		
×	×	×		×	×	×
×	×	×		×	×	×
designers		year			×	×
Marco Bedeschi		2007				
Michele Santandrea						
×	×	×		×	×	×
×	×	×		×	×	×

Joe Badile, Creative Man

Giorgio Paolinelli
+39 349 777 61 50
joebadile.altervista.org
joebadile@gmail.com

×××

agency/design studio		client		art director	
Joe Badile		Giorgio Paolinelli		Giorgio Paolinelli	
×	×	×	×	×	×
×	×	×	×	×	×
designer		year			
Giorgio Paolinelli		2007			
×	×	×	×		×
×	×	×	×	×	×

xx

agency/design studio	client	art directors
IAKI- marketing esperienziale	Net Center S.r.l	Eleonora Bottalico; Carlos Coll; Juan Carlos Lopez

×   ×   ×   ×   ×

designer	year	
Eleonora Bottalico	2006/2007	

×   ×   ×   ×   ×

×   ×   ×   ×   ×

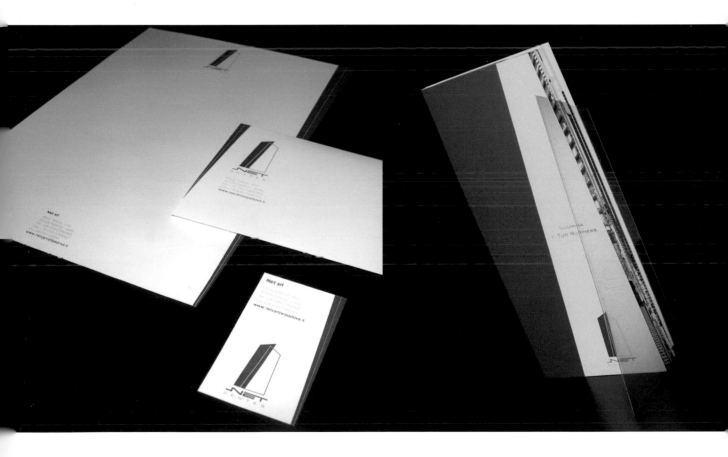

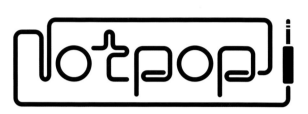

××

agency/design studio		client		art director	
Ikon Advertising		Not Pop		Valerio Galli	
×	×	×		×	×
×	×	×	×	×	×
designer		year		×	×
Emanuela Esposito		2007		×	×
×	×	×	×	×	×
×	×	×	×	×	×

notpop

ELECTRONIC NUJAZZ JOURNEY

LUCIANO ZANONI **KEYBOARDS**
CARLO MICHELI **SAXOPHONE**
PIERPAOLO RANIERI **ELETTRIC BASS**
STEFANO MARAZZI **DRUMS**

SEASON 2006·2007

MP *organizza*

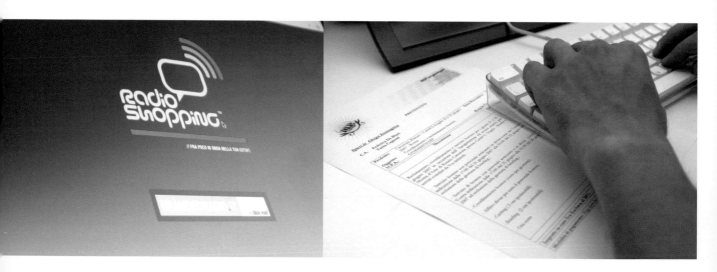

❯220❮

××

agency/design studio	client	art director
Ikon Advertising	Radio Shopping MP Organizza	Valerio Galli

× × × × ×

× × × × × ×

designer	year		
Emanuela Esposito	2007	×	×

× × × × × ×

× × × × × ×

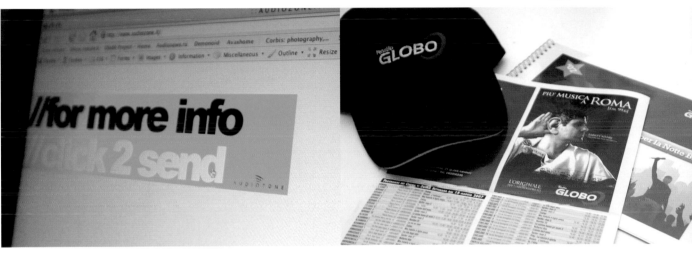

> 221 <

xxxxxxxxxxxxxxxxxxxxxxxxxxxxxxxxxxxxxxxxxxxxxxxxxxxxxxxxxxxxxxxxxxxxxxxxxxx

agency/design studio		client		art director	
Ikon Advertising		Audiozone Radio Globo		Valerio Galli	
×	×	×	×	×	×
×	×	×	×	×	×
designer		year		×	×
Emanuela Esposito		2007			
×	×	×	×	×	×
×	×	×	×	×	×

xxx

agency/design studio	client	art director
Kalimera	Off Limits	Kalimera

× × × × × ×

× × × × ×

designer	× ×	year	× ×	×
Kalimera		2008		×

× × × × × ×

× × × × × ×

xx

agency/design studio	client	art director
Ikon Advertising	**Ikon Advertising**	**Valerio Galli**

designer	year
Emanuela Esposito	**2007**

agency/design studio		client			art director	
Gumdesign		**Comune di Massa**			**Gumdesign**	
×	×	×	×	×	×
×	×	×	×	×	×
designer		year			×	×
Gumdesign		**2007**				
×	×	×	×	×	×
×	×	×	×	×	×

×××

agency/design studio	client	art director
Gianni Rossi Studio	ACAB	Gianni Rossi

× × × × × ×

× × × × ×

designer	year	
Gianni Rossi	1999	

× × × × ×

× × × × ×

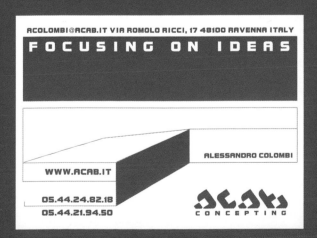

agency/design studio		client		art director	
Gianni Rossi Studio		Revolver		Gianni Rossi	
×	×	×		×	×	×
×	×	×		×	×	×
designer		year			
Gianni Rossi		2002		×	×
×	×	×		×	×	×
×	×	×		×	×	×

Marathon
enigma a Manhattan

Paolo Maria Spina per REVOLVER
e Stefano Stefani per ATELIER presentano:

un film di
AMIR NADERI

Un film di: Amir Naderi Interpreti: Sara Paul, Trevor Moore, Rebecca Nelson Produzione: Amir Naderi – Alphaville NYC In coproduzione con: Revolver Bologna – Roma, gruppo L'Atelier - Firenze Fotografia: Michael Simmonds Montaggio: Amir Naderi, Donald O'Ceilleachair

www.revolverteam.com

xxx

agency/design studio	client	art director
Marina Turci	Associazione Culturale Mare in Italy	Marina Turci

designer	year
Marina Turci	2004/2008

××

agency/design studio	client	art director
2mlab	**Aprimondo**	**Mirko Magnani**

designer	year
Mirko Magnani	**2005**

›231‹

×××

agency/design studio	client	art director
2mlab	**Casa Adesso**	**Mirko Magnani**

× × × × × ×

× × × × ×

designer	year	
Mirko Magnani	**2006**	

× × × × × ×

× × × × × ×

agency/design studio	client	art director
Gianni Rossi Studio	Ships	Gianni Rossi

designer	year	
Gianni Rossi	2007	

xxx

agency/design studio	client	art director
Gianni Rossi Studio	**Wp Lavori in Corso**	**Luca Caccioni**

designer	year
Gianni Rossi	**2003**

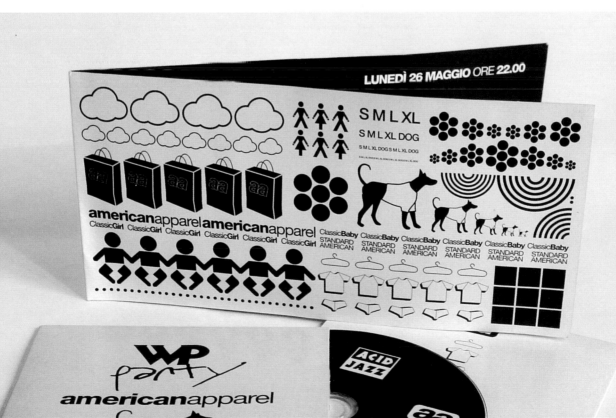

xx

agency/design studio		client	art director		
Gianni Rossi Studio		**Portobello's Vintage Bar**	**Gianni Rossi**		
x	x	x	x	x	x
x	x	x	x	x	x
designer	x	x	x	x	x
Gianni Rossi		year			
		2007	x		x
x	x	x	x	x	x
x	x	x	x	x	x

agency/design studio	client	art director
Gianni Rossi Studio	**Dejavu Records**	**Gianni Rossi**

×	×	×	×	×	×
×	×	×	×	×	×

designer	year	
Gianni Rossi	**2004**	

×	×	×	×	×	×
×	×	×	×	×	×

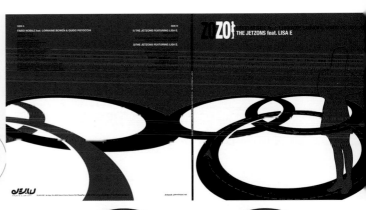

© 2005 Tam Tam Studio Recordings

xxx

agency/design studio	client	art director
Gianni Rossi Studio	**Tam Tam Studio Recordings**	**Gianni Rossi**

designer	year	web programmer
Gianni Rossi	**2005-2008**	**Simone Medri**

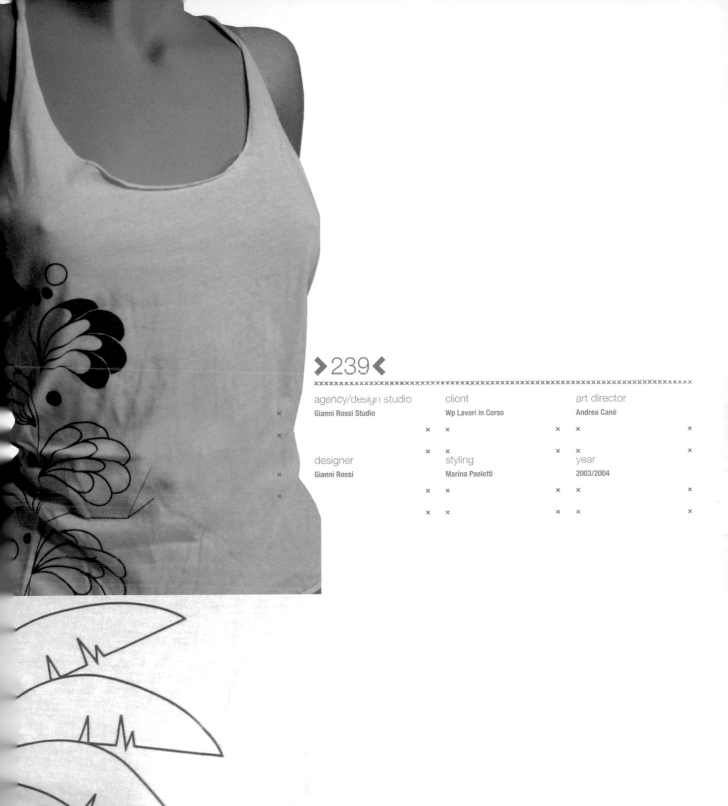

>239<

agency/design studio
Gianni Rossi Studio

cliont
Wp Lavori in Corso

art director
Andrea Canè

designer
Gianni Rossi

styling
Marina Paoletti

year
2003/2004

××

agency/design studio	client	art director
Gianni Rossi Studio	Wp Lavori in Corso	Andrea Canè

×   × ×   × ×   ×

designer	styling	year
Gianni Rossi	Marina Paoletti	2003/2004

×   × ×   × ×   ×

×   × ×   × ×   ×

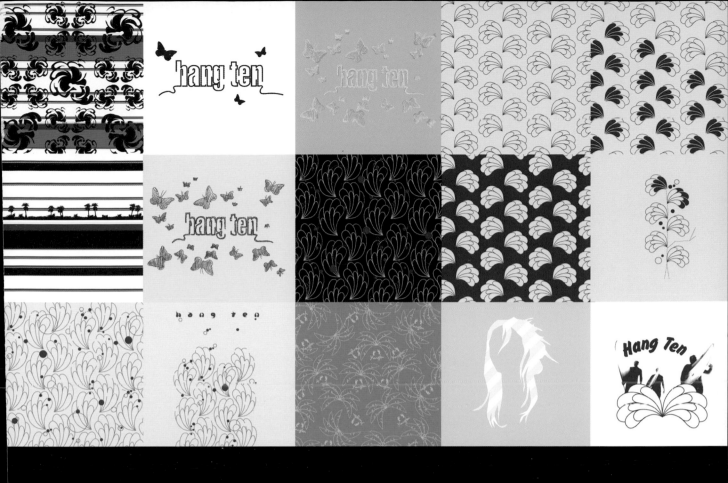

agency/design studio	client	art director
Fabbricando	**Multisala Aladdin**	**Claudia Fabbri**

× × × × × ×

× ×

designer	year	
Claudia Fabbri	**2000/2006**	× ×

× × × × ×

× × × × × ×

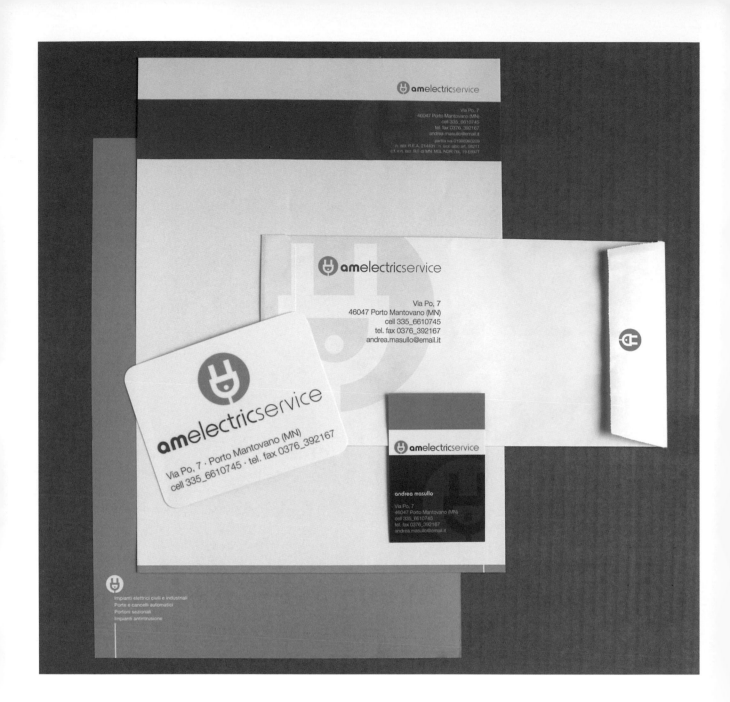

××

agency/design studio		client		art director	
Copiaincolla		**AM Electric Service**		**Cesare Tonolli**	
×	×	×	×	×	
	×	×	×	×	×
designer		year			
Silvia Pavesi		**2007**			
				×	×
×	×	×	×	×	
×	×	×	×	×	

xxxxxxxxxxxxxxxxxxxxxxxxxxxxxxxxxxxxxxxxxxxxxxxxxxxxxxxxxxxxxxxxxx

agency/design studio		client		art director	
Turconi&Co		**Mizar srl**		**Mario Turconi**	
×	×	×	×	×	
×	×	×	×	×	×
designer		year			
Alessia Gatti		**2006**		×	×
×	×	×	×	×	
×	×	×	×	×	×

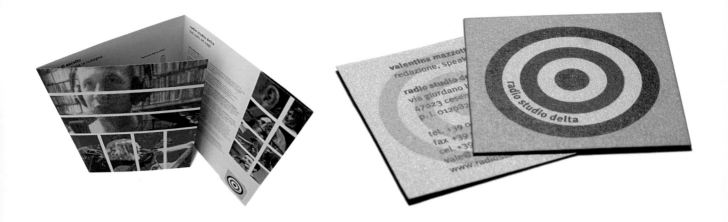

×××

agency/design studio	client	art director
Fabbricando	**Radio Studio Delta**	**Claudia Fabbri**

designer	year
Claudia Fabbri	**2003/2005**

×××

agency/design studio
Fabbricando

client
Radio Studio Delta

art director
Claudia Fabbri

×   ×   ×   ×   ×   ×

×   ×   ×   ×   ×

designer   ×   year
Claudia Fabbri   2003/2005
                            ×

×   ×   ×   ×   ×

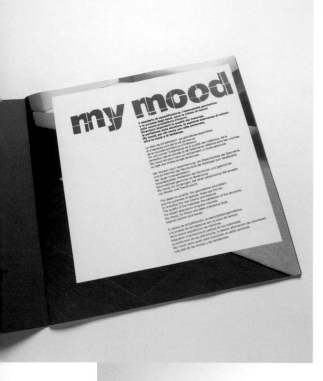

xxx

agency/design studio	client	art director	
Kalimera	Ceramiche Supergres	Kalimera	
×	×	×	×
×	×	×	×
designer	year	×	×
Kalimera	2007		
×	×	×	×
×	×	×	×

×××

agency/design studio	client	art director
2mlab	Hotel Casali	Mirko Magnani

× × × × ×

× × × × ×

designer	year
Mirko Magnani	2005

× × × × × ×

× × × × × ×

××

agency/design studio	client	art director
Cento per Cento	Furla	Pier Paolo Pitacco

× × × × × ×

× × × × ×

designer	year	× ×
Francesco Ponzi	2001	

× × × × × ×

× × × × × ×

××

agency/design studio	client	art director
2mlab	Twenty	Mirko Magnani

× × × × × ×

× × × × ×

designer	year		
Mirko Magnani	2005		

× × × × ×

× × × × ×

agency/design studio	client	art director
Cento per Cento	Ermenegildo Zegna	Pier Paolo Pitacco

designer	year
Francesco Ponzi	2001

agency/design studio   client   art directors
Unleaded   **Materis Paints Italia** **Nicola Lattanzi**
                                                         Riccardo Danesi

x   x   x   x   x   x

x   x   x   x   x   x
designer   year
Nicola Lattanzi   **2006**   x

x   x   x   x   x   x

x   x   x   x   x   x

xxxxxxxxxxxxxxxxxxxxxxxxxxxxxxxxxxxxxxxxxxxxxxxxxxxxxxxxxxxxxxxxxxxxxxxxxxxxxxxxxxxxxxxxxxxxxx

agency/design studio	client	art director
FK Design Srl	Antoniana Caffè Srl	Giovanni Frison

designer	year
Giovanni Frison	2007

××

agency/design studio	client	art director
Fabbricando	**Fabbricando**	**Claudia Fabbri**
×	× ×	× × ×
×	× ×	× × ×
designer	year	
Claudia Fabbri	**2002/2006**	× ×
×	× ×	× × ×
×	× ×	× × ×

agency/design studio	client	art director
Marina Turci	Beach Games srl	Marina Turci

designer	year
Marina Turci	1990/2008

xx

agency/design studio	client	art director
Linke	**PuntoMercato**	**Rossella Lezzi**

designer	year	
Rossella Lezzi	**2005**	

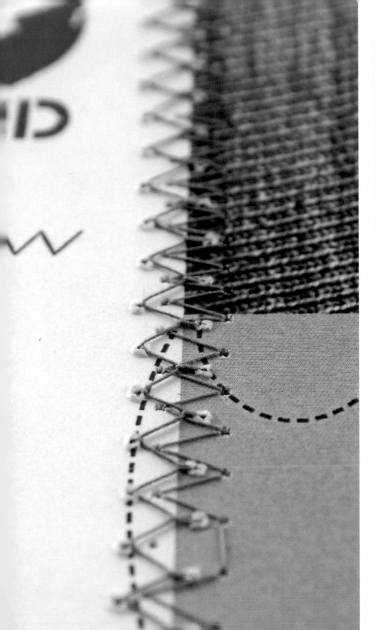

×××

agency/design studio	client	art director
Temecula design	**Syb products srl**	**Cristiano de Veroli**

designer	year	
Cristiano de Veroli	**2007**	

xx

agency/design studio	client	art directors
Cambiamenti	**Feste Medioevali di Brisighella**	**Carlo Zauli**
		Jan Guerrini

× × × ×

× × × ×

designer	year	
Jan Guerrini	**2003/2008**	×

× × × × ×

× × × × ×

xxx

agency/design studio	client	art director
Temecula design	**Elena Chiesa**	**Cristiano de Veroli**

designer	year
Cristiano de Veroli	**2007**

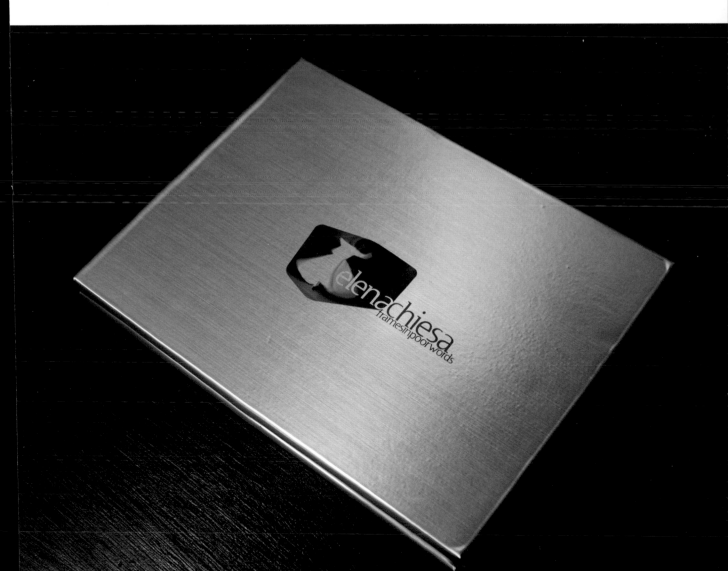

agency/design studio	client	art director
Cambiamenti	Corona	Laura Zavalloni

designer	year	
Laura Zavalloni	2007/2008	

agency/design studio	client	art director
Basso grafica e design	Everybody	Giuliano Basso

designer	year
Giovanni Basso	1999

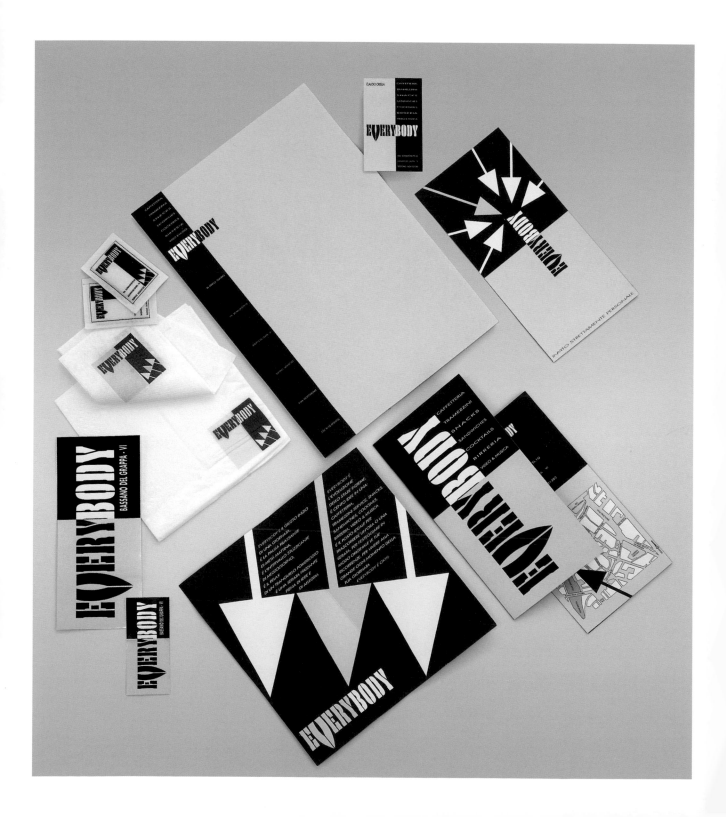

xx

agency/design studio	client	art director
Fachiro Strategic Design	**Ekma ricerche srl**	**Amedeo Palazzi**

designer	year
Silvia Grisanti	**2007**

Galleria Buenos Aires 1
20124 Milano
T +39 02 66809669
F +39 02 6685791
info@ekmaricerche.com
www.ekmaricerche.com

xx

agency/design studio	client	art director
Cento per cento	Azienda agricola Tenuta Arpineto	Pier Paolo Pitacco

×   × ×   × ×   ×

×   × ×   × ×   ×

designer	year	
Pier Paolo Pitacco	2001	

×   × ×   ×   ×

×   × ×   ×   ×

xxx

agency/design studio	client	art director
Cento per cento	**Montegrappa**	**Pier Paolo Pitacco**

designer	year
Francesco Ponzi	**2003 - 2004**

××

agency/design studio	client	art director	
Temecula design	Misterbike freerider shop	Cristiano de Veroli	
×	× ×	× ×	×
×	× ×	× ×	×
designer	year	×	×
Cristiano de Veroli	2006		
×	× ×	× ×	×
×	× ×	× ×	×

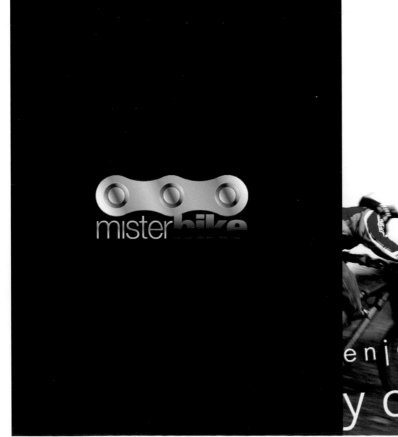

×××

agency/design studio	client	art director
Fachiro Strategic Design	Comune di Mantova	Amedeo Palazzi

× × × × ×

× × × ×

designer	year
Amedeo Palazzi	2002

× × × × ×

× × × × ×

××

agency/design studio	client	art directors
Matitegiovanotte	**Bisanzio Software**	**Giovanni Pizzigati**
		Barbara Longiardi
×	× ×	×

designers	year
Barbara Longiardi	**2006**
Giovanni Pizzigati	

xxxxxxxxxxxxxxxxxxxxxxxxxxxxxxxxxxxxxxxxxxxxxxxxxxxxxxxxxxxxxxxxxxxxxxxxxxxxxxxxxxxxxxxxxxxxxx

agency/design studio		client		art director	
2mlab		**Officina Costume**		**Mirko Magnani**	
x	x	x		x	x
x	x	x		x	x
designer		year		x	x
Mirko Magnani		**2006**			
x	x	x		x	x
x	x	x		x	x

xxxxxxxxxxxxxxxxxxxxxxxxxxxxxxxxxxxxxxxxxxxxxxxxxxxxxxxxxxxxxxxxxxxxxxx

agency/design studio	client	art director
Fachiro Strategic Design	**IES Italiana Energia e Servizi spa**	**Amedeo Palazzi**

designer	year
Riccardo Braccaioli	**2004/2007**

agency/design studio	client	art director
Fachiro Strategic Design	Due minuti per il partito democratico Libera associazione online	Amedeo Palazzi

designer	year
Amedeo Palazzi	2007

B. LODA RMX

MC1 Basic

synthonic

SYNTHONIC REC. VIA VOLGA 18/a 48020 SAVIO DI CERVIA RAVENNA ITALY
PHONE/FAX: +39 0544 928093 www.paoloscotti.com E-MAIL: info@paoloscotti.com

xxxxxxxxxxxxxxxxxxxxxxxxxxxxxxxxxxxxxxxxxxxxxxxxxxxxxxxxxxxx

agency/design studio	client	art director
Gianni Rossi Studio	Synthonic Records	Gianni Rossi

× × × × × ×

× × × × ×

designer	year	
Gianni Rossi	2006	

× × × × × × ×

× × × × × × ×

>281<

××

agency/design studio		client		art director	
Studio Chiesa & Officina Visuale		Marcegaglia		Rossella Roncaia	
×	×	×	×	×	×
×	×	×	×	×	×
designers		year			
Sara Ronconi; Cinzia Casoni; Monica Gordin		2001/2007	×		×
×	×	×	×	×	×
×	×	×	×	×	×

Art Center College Library
1700 Lida Street
Pasadena, CA 91103

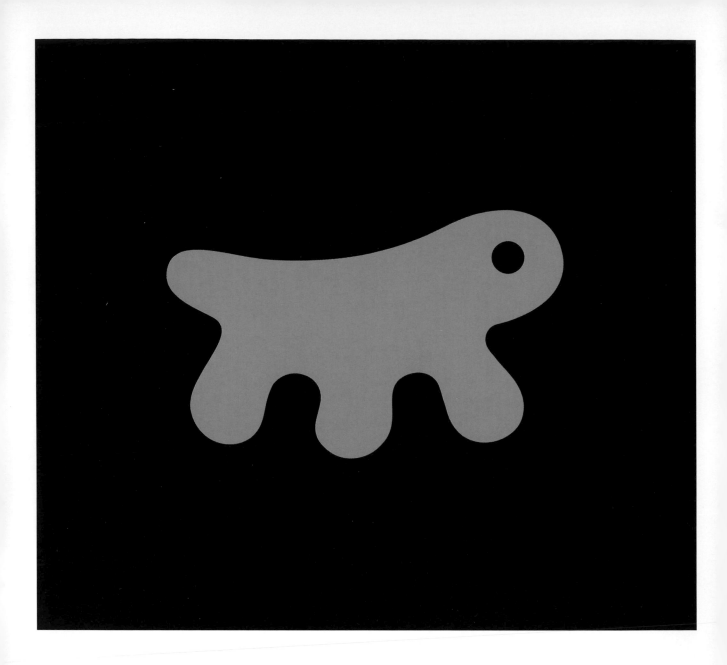

××

agency/design studio	client	design director
Univisual - Milan	Ferplast (pet products_ international company leader)	Gaetano Grizzanti
×	× ×	× ×
×	× ×	× ×
designers	year	
Gaetano Grizzanti; Sara Villa; Maurizio Strippoli	2005	× ×
×	× ×	× ×
×	× ×	× ×

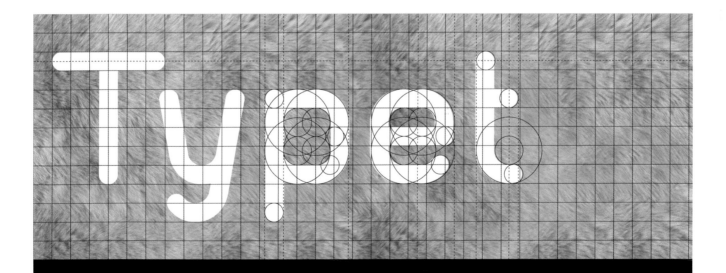

AÀÂÄBCDEÉÊËFGHIÍÎÏJKLMNOÓÔÖPQRSTUÚÛÜVWXYZ

aàâäbcdeéêëfghiíîïjklmnoóôöpqrstuúûüvwxyz

1234567890 [,.:;!?"'+=*°&£$€¥@®©]

ferplast
new pet generation

>284<

×××

agency/design studio	client	art director
Gianni Rossi Studio	Dejavu Records Commodo Depot Inc	Gianni Rossi

designer	year
Gianni Rossi	2007

> 285 <

xxxxxxxxxxxxxxxxxxxxxxxxxxxxxxxxxxxxxxxxxxxxxxxxxxxxxxxxxxxxxxxx

agency/design studio		client		art director	
Gianni Rossi Studio		Commodo Depot Inc.		Gianni Rossi	
×	×	×	×	×	×
×	×	×	×	×	×
designer		year		×	×
Gianni Rossi		2007		×	×
×	×	×	×	×	×
×	×	×	×	×	×

×××

agency/design studio	client	design director
Univisual - Milan	Fandis (engineering company)	Gaetano Grizzanti

× × × × × ×

designers	year
Gaetano Grizzanti; Sara Villa; Maurizio Strippoli	2006

× × × × × ×

× × × × × ×

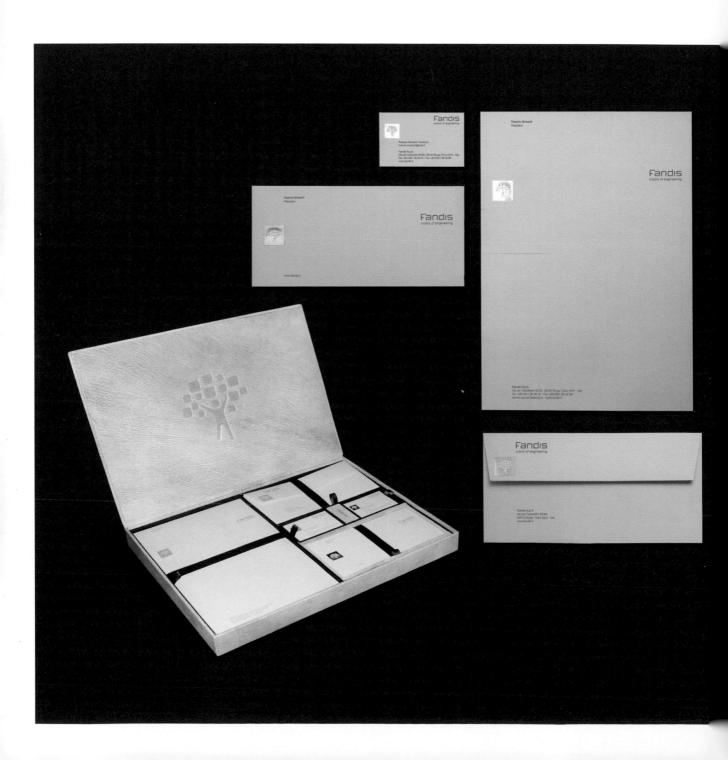

Fandistype

a b c d e F g h i j k l m
n o p q r s t u v w x y z
@ & % $ £ ß ? ! { [. . , : :] }
1 2 3 4 5 6 7 8 9 0

288

xxxxxxxxxxxxxxxxxxxxxxxxxxxxxxxxxxxxxxxxxxxxxxxxxxxxxxxxxxxxxxxxxxxxxxxxx

agency/design studio		client		art director	
br&a		**Vismaravetro**		**Bruno Romano**	
×	×	×		×	×	×
×	×	×		×	×	×
designer		year			×	×
Ferruccio Fumagalli		**2006/2007**			×	×
×	×	×		×	×	×
×	×	×		×	×	×

DJV 2000038 **ENZO**
SCOPPA
QUINTET
STANDARD

SIDA A:
1. THE END OF LOVE AFFAIR - (Edward C. Redding) 7'35"
2. EAST OF THE SUN - (Brooks Bowman) 6'11"
3. FIVE HUNDRED MILES - (Chick Corea) 7'19"
SIDE B:
1. THIS I DIG OF YOU - (Hank Mobley) 4'48"
2. BLUE ZONE - (Enzo Scoppa) 6'32"
3. EU E VOCE - (Carlos Lyra- Vinicious de Moraes) 6'28"

Enzo Scoppa tenor and soprano* saxophone
Gianbattista Gioia flugehorn
Claudio Colasazza piano
Francesco Puglisi bass
Amedeo Ariano drums
Arrangements

Massimo Simonetti
D'Aquino
ni Rossi Studio
a studios

rding of the Scopp
o rarely record u
ecious-but-dated
to the awarenes
ers of this publ
imilar to those
opinion of

tight hole
d. Righth
ble ori
rara-
one
The

> 289 <

×××

agency/design studio	client	art director	
Gianni Rossi Studio	Dejavu Records	Gianni Rossi	
×	×	×	×	×	×
×	×	×	×	×	×
designer	year	×	×
Gianni Rossi	2007	×	×
×	×	×	×	×
×	×	×	×	×	×

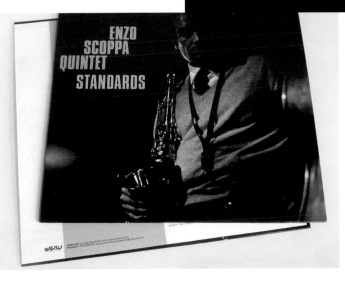

agency/design studio	client	design director
Univisual - Milan	Aethra (telecommunication)	Gaetano Grizzanti

designers	year
Gaetano Grizzanti; Sara Villa; Maurizio Strippoli	2007

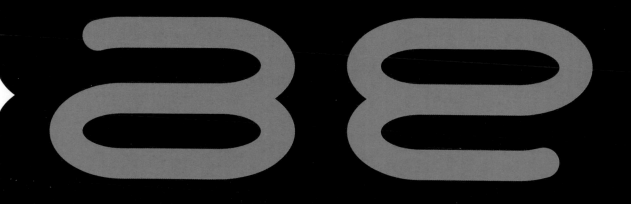

aethratype

aàbcdeèéfghiìjklmn
oòpqrstuùvwxyz
(-:.;,?!=@""&><°%+$€)
0123456789

❯292❮

×××

agency/design studio	client	design director
Univisual - Milan	STS Elettronica (alarm systems)	Gaetano Grizzanti

designers	year
Gaetano Grizzanti; Maurizio Strippoli; Sara Villa	2005

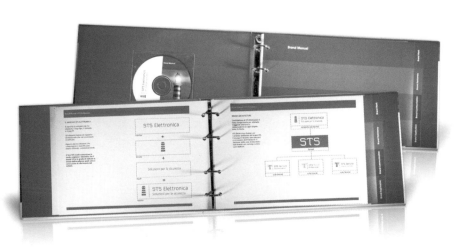

agency/design studio	client	art director
Kalimera	**Tavola Calda Board Shop**	**Kalimera**

designer	year	
Kalimera	**2007**	

xxxxxxxxxxxxxxxxxxxxxxxxxxxxxxxxxxxxxxxxxxxxxxxxxxxxxxxxxxxxxxxxxxxxxxxxxxxxxxx

agency/design studio		client		art director
Kalimera		Tavola Calda Board Shop		Kalimera

designer		year	
Kalimera		2005	

400 gr	BLOMOR
BUILDING	CHEAPO
DEAD MEAT	FRAV
FURIOUS CLOTHING	HELLS BELLS
ILLEGITIMATE	NOODLE PARK
PHARMACY INDUSTRY	RADICAL DIVERSITY
REVOLUTION	SUPER SUNGLASSES
	SEA SURFER BY KRONOBERG

WELCOME TO MY HOUSE

WELCOME TO MY HOUSE

DEAD MEAT

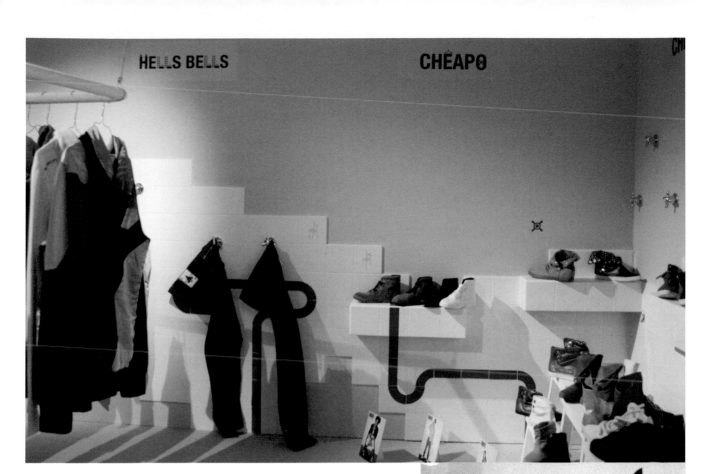

400 gr.

×××

agency/design studio	client	design director
Univisual - Milan	VistaSì (optical store chain)	Gaetano Grizzanti

designers	year
Gaetano Grizzanti; Maurizio Strippoli	2003

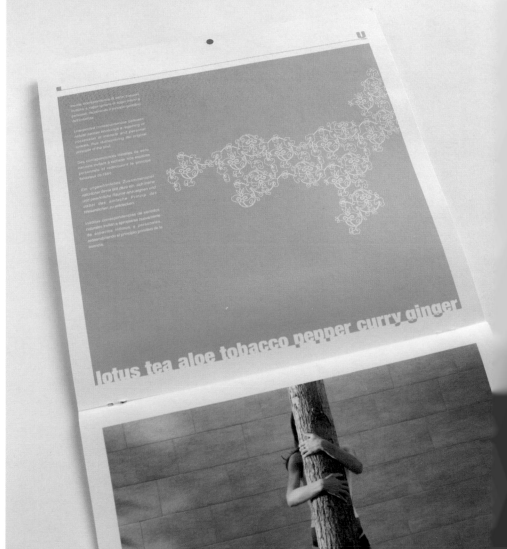

×××

agency/design studio	client	art director
Kalimera	Ceramiche Supergres	Kalimera

×	×	×	×	×	×
×	×	×	×	×

designer	year			
Kalimera	2005			

×	×	×	×	×	×
×	×	×	×	×

> 304 <
×××

agency/design studio		client		art director	
FK Design Srl		IDD		Giovanni Frison	
×	×	×		×	×
×	×	×		×	×
designer		year			
Giovanni Frison		2006		×	×
×	×	×		×	×
×	×	×		×	×

ΔRC2/

ARC27 LABORATORIO DI ARCHITETTURA

×××

agency/design studio		client		art director		
Marina Turci		Arc27		Marina Turci		
	×	×		×	×	×
	×	×		×	×	×
designer		year				
Marina Turci		2007				
				×		×
	×	×		×	×	×
	×	×		×	×	×

xx

agency/design studio		client		art director	
Dinamo Project		Dinamo Project		Marco Bedeschi	
×	×	×	×	×	×
×	×	×	×	×	×
designers		year			
Marco Bedeschi		2007			
Michele Santandrea				×	×
×	×	×	×	×	×
×	×	×	×	×	×

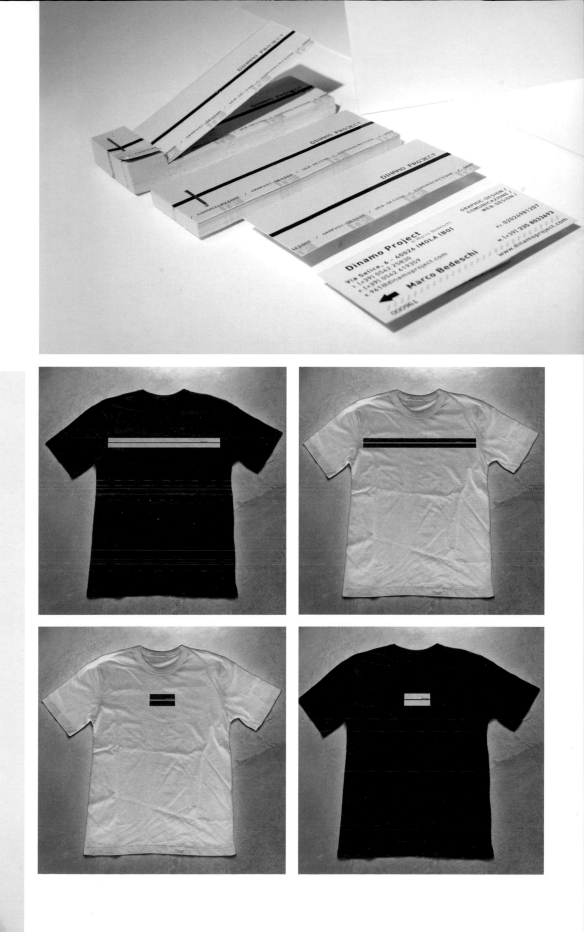

xxx

agency/design studio	client	art director
Kalimera	Now by Persona	Kalimera
×	× ×	× × ×
×	× ×	× × ×
designer	year	
Kalimera	2007/2008	
		× ×
×	× ×	× × ×
×	× ×	× × ×

N.O.W.
NATION OF WOMEN
BY PERSONA

NOW
CHANGE
INSIZE
info@personamr.it

xxxxxxxxxxxxxxxxxxxxxxxxxxxxxxxxxxxxxxxxxxxxxxxxxxxxxxxxxxxxxxxxxxxxxxxx

agency/design studio	client	design director
Univisual - Milan	Targa Infomobility (Infomobility Telematic Services)	Gaetano Grizzanti
×	× ×	× ×
×	× ×	× ×
designers	year	
Gaetano Grizzanti; Sara Villa; Maurizio Strippoli	2007	× ×
×	× ×	× ×
×	× ×	× ×

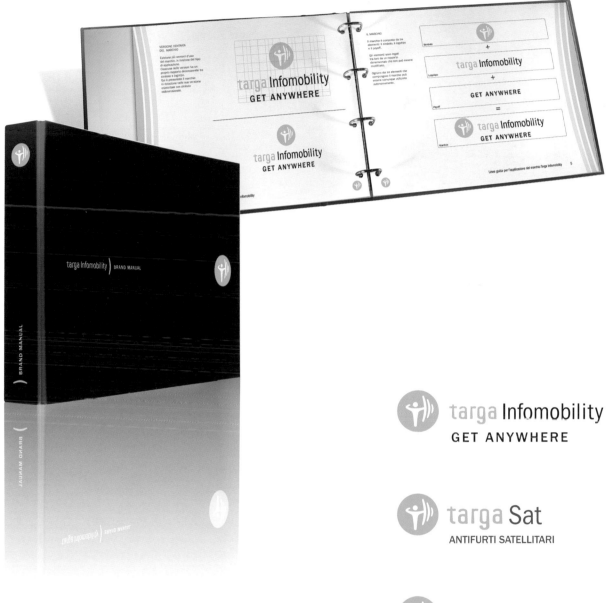

targa Infomobility
GET ANYWHERE

targa Sat
ANTIFURTI SATELLITARI

targa Sat
ANTIFURTI SATELLITARI

targa Traffic
VIABILITÀ IN TEMPO REALE

targa Voice
INFORMAZIONI VOCE E SMS

xx

agency/design studio	client	art director
Longe Design	Emap Performance TV (Smash Hits!)	Heric Longe Abramo

x   x   x   x   x   x

designer	year	
Heric Longe Abramo	2006	

ENERGISE!

Short'N'Strong

INDEX OF AGENCIES
AND WORKS

xxxxxxxxxxxxxxxxxxxxxxxxxxxxxxxxx

Art Center College Library
1700 Lida Street
Pasadena, CA 91103

Index of agencies and works

Dinamo Project_Imola
961@dinamoproject.com
www.dinamoproject.com
214.215.306

Doppiazeta_Modena
doppiazeta@libero.it
206

Due mani non bastano_Milano
info@duemaninonbastano.it
www.duemaninonbastano.it
201.202

Alexander Egger_Vienna
alex@satellitesmistakenforstars.com
www.satellitesmistakenforstars.com
66.68.126.148.151.172

Equilibrisospesi_Ravenna
info@equilibrisospesi.com
www.equilibrisospesi.com
204.205.207

Esseblu_Milano
info@esseblu.it
www.@esseblu.it
200

Fabbricando_Cesena_Fc
info@fabbricando.com
www.fabbricando.com
46.47.49.50.80.242.247.249.258

Fachiro Strategic Design_Mantova
amedeo@fachiro.com
www.fachiro.com
208.209.210.211.212.269
273.276.277

Fk Design Srl_Treviso
info@fkdesign.it
www.fkdesign.it
64.65.72.76.78.81.257.304

Joe Badile_Lucca
joebadile@gmail.com
www.joebadile.altervista.org
216

Gumdesign_Viareggio
info@gumdesign.it
www.gumdesign.it
224

Happycentro_Verona
info@happycentro.it
www.happycentro.it
12.15.16

IAKI_Milano
citofonare@iaki.it
www.iaki.it
217

Ikon Advertising_Roma
info@ikon-adv.com
www.ikon-adv.com
218.220.221.223

Index of agencies and works

Startmedia_Napoli
info@startmedia.it
www. startmedia.it
36

Stockbridge.it_Bologna
info@stockbridge.it
www.stockbridge.it
22

Studio Chiesa
& Officina Visuale_Milano
staff@officinavisuale.it
www.officinavisuale.it
281

StudioGuida_Napoli
firstcontact@studioguida.net
www.studioguida.net
193

Studio Priori_Milano
info@studiopriori.com
www.studiopriori.com
86.88

Studiosancisi_Pesaro
info@studiosancisi.it
www.studiosancisi.it
38.156.190.191.192

Temecula Design_Roma
info@temecula.it
www.temecula.it
114.115.263.265.272

Turconi&Co_Como
info@turconicompany.it
www.turconicompany.it
245

Univisual_Milano
mail@univisual.it
www.univisual.it
58.282.286.290.292.300.310

Unleaded_Massarosa
info@unleaded.it
www.unleaded.it
256

Up!_Paris
staff@up-studio.org
www.up-studio.org
44.45,298

X-ray_Bergamo
xray@xray-net.it
www.xray-net.it
70

Zetalab_Milano
info@zetalab.com
www.zetalab.com
8.62.96

Art Center College Library
1700 Lida Street
Pasadena, CA 91103